BUDDHISM IN INDIA

BUDDHISM IN INDIA

From the Sixth Century B.C. to the Third Century A.D.

Ashok Kumar Anand

Buddhism in India: From the Sixth Century B.C. to the Third Century A.D.

ISBN: 81-212-0506-9

Reprinted in 2012 in India by
Gyan Publishing House
23, Main Ansari Road, Daryaganj,
New Delhi - 110002
Phone : 23282060, 23261060
Fax : (011) 23285914
E-mail : books@gyanbooks.com
Website: gyanbooks.com

Printed at: G. Print Process, Delhi

Dedicated to
Profound Memory of

Dr. Yogendra Mishra
(31.3.1920—21.4.1993)

ROMAN EQUIVALENTS OF NAGARI LETTERS

अ	a	आ	ā	इ	i	ई	ī
उ	u	ऊ	ū	ऋ	ṛ	ए	e
ऐ	ai	ओ	o	औ	au		
क्	k	ख्	kh	ग्	g	घ्	gh
ङ	ṅ	च्	c	छ्	ch	ज्	j
झ्	jh	ञ्	ñ	ट्	ṭ	ठ्	ṭh
ड्	ḍ	द्	ḍh	ण्	ṇ	त्	t
थ्	th	द्	d	ध्	dh	न्	n
प्	p	फ्	ph	ब्	b	भ्	bh
म्	m	य्	y	र्	r	ल्	l
व्	v	श्	ś	ष्	ṣ	स्	s
ह्	h	क्ष्	kṣ	त्र्	tr	ज्ञ्	jñ

Anusvaraṁ Visargaḥ

Abbreviations

Ang. Nik.	Aṅgutara Nikāya
ASI	Archaeological Survey of India, Report
AV	Atharvaveda
BDG	Bengal District Gazetters and Bihar District Gazetters
CHB	Comprehensive History of Bihar
CHI	Cambridge History of India
CII	Corpus Inscriptionum Indicarum
DV	Dīpa Vaṁśa
JASB	Journal of the Asiatic Society of Bengal
JBORS	Journal of the Bihar and Orissa Research Society
JIH	Journal of the Indian History
JRAS	Journal of the Royal Asiatic Society
KA	Kautilya's Arthaśāstra
MASI	Memoirs of the Archaeological Survey of India
Majjh. Nik.	Majjhima Nikāya
MRE	Minor Rock Edict
MV	Mahāvaṁśa
NIA	New Indian Antiquary
P	Page
PE	Pillar Edict
PHAI	Political History of Ancient India
QJMS	Quarterly Journal of the Mythic Society

RE	Rock Edict
RV	Ṛgveda
SBE	Sacred Books of the East
SN	Samyutta Nikāya
Tr. (tr.)	Translation
Vol.	Volume
ZDMG	Zeitschrift der Deutschen Morgenlandichen Gesellschaft

Preface

In recent years regional studies have become more significant for the social scientists and especially to the historians who claim to trace "history from the below." In the present work it has been endeavoured to see Buddhism in its entirety laying some-what lesser emphasis on philosophy. It is because much has already been written on this aspect.

Bihar has ever been the land of greater importance so for as the history of Buddhism is concerned. It is because Gautama became 'Buddha' — The enlightened in this region. Every year, students from Thailand, Tibet and Japan come to Bihar and they readily accept to study Buddhism. All these developments enabled me to think and rethink the origin, development and spread of Buddhism in Bihar. Bihar played greater role in the spread of the philosophy and its main tenets in India and outside. On philosophical aspect, several works appear to be in existence but in its entirety a few works may be taken into account.

The present work consists of six chapters for which data have been collected mainly from literary evidences. In chapter II, extensive study has been made to trace the origin of Buddhism in Bihar in its socio-political and geographical settings. In this chapter it has also been largely discussed as to whose interest did this newly found religion serve i.e. the rulers or the subjects. Traditionally, Buddhism is interpreted as a potent reaction against the Brahmanic cult. But the present work speaks more about the socio-political environment and thus the growth of Buddhism was a historical necessity.

In chapter III, the development of Buddhist art has been traced. Buddhist art received its, incentives from a king like

Aśoka but essentially it owes its origin to the enthusiasm and efforts of the Buddhist laity.

The chapter IV deals with the developments of Buddhism in the time of Aśoka. In this chapter, it has been attempted to raise some basic controversies regarding Asoka's conversion to Buddhism and what measures did he take to propagate this religion in India and other neighbouring countries. Aśoka has, in many ways been regarded as the representative of his age. To what extent Buddhism did serve the cause of the ruler and the society as well ?

In chapter V, condition of Buddhism during the period between the fall of the Mauryas and rise of the Kusana kings has been judged. The period under study is important for two reasons; one noted for the transformation in the history of Buddhism and secondly, with the fall of the Mauryas, Brahmaṇism again was raising its head.

In the course of historical development, the break away of Buddhism into different sects could not be checked. In chapter VI, transformation of Buddhism into different schools has been estimated with special emphasis on the socio-political and economic environment that made the cause of transformation inevitable.

Now it becomes all the more necessary to acknowledge the co-operation extended by a group of scholar who time and again helped me to complete this work.

This book could not have assumed its present shape without the able guidance of my Ph. D. supervisor. **Dr. Shatrughna Sharan Singh**, Reader, Dept. of Ancient Indian History and Archaelogy, Patna University. I cannot unburden myself of his debt by giving any amount of thanks to him.

I am greatly indebted to the late **Dr. Yogendra Mishra** (1920-1993). Formerly Prof. and Head of the Dept. of History, Patna University, a historian of great repute, who cound not see the book published, but who had always inspired and guided me to complete this work.

It will be an act of ungratefulness if I pass on without acknowledging the help of Professor **Brajdeo Prasad Roy,** Head of the Dept. of Ancient Indian History and Archaeology, Patana University. I am highly obliged to **Dr. Chittaranjan Prasad Sinha,** Director, K.P. Jayaswal Research Institute for his help regarding access to journals and valuable sources.

Dr. Rajendra Ram, Professor of History, Patna University and **Dr. (Mrs.) Jayshri Mishra,** Reader in History, Magadh Mahila College, Patna University deserve my sincere thanks, who offered helpful criticisms during the course of research.

I am also thankful to **Dr. Arun Kumar Mishra,** Reader, Dept. of History, Bihar University, and **Dr. Jayadeva Mishra,** Lecturer in Ancient Indian History and Archaeology, Patna University, for their valuable suggestions.

My friend, **Dr. Akhilesh Kumar** helped me a lot during the course of study. I have also received valuable suggestions from **Dr. Premendra Priyadarshi, Dr. Rajiv Kamal,** and many more. My sincere thanks are due to them.

Apart from these individuals, institutions have also helped me by allowing access to the sources. I am highly indebted to the National Library Calcutta, Patna University litrary, Sinha Library, R.K. Misson Library, Bihar State Archives Library, K.P. Jayaswal Research Institute and the Bihar Research Institute, all situated at Patna.

I am specially indebted to my parents, **Shri Chaturbuj Singh** and **Smt. Savitri Devi** whose affection and sacrifices have always encouraged me to tide over the rough weathers.

I woe my sincere thanks to my wife **Neelam** who appreciated the value of my time while I was writing the manuscript, and left me aloof from homely affairs. What more a scholor can expect from his wife ?

Last but not the least. I place on record my gratitude to those great savants in the field whose writings have been extensively utilized in preparing the thesis.

Finally, I am grateful to publisher without whose help this book would not have come into print.

Patna **Ashok Kumar Anand**

Contents

Chapter I

Introduction

Bihar has played a very important role in the history of India since remote past. Bihar in ancient times was both Greece and Rome for India. It was a centre of religious and cultural movements which define the contours of cultural topography of India. It was also the hub of political activities and fountain spring of political ideas and institutions which shaped the juridic personality and political culture of the country down the ages. From here were generated the art currents which soon enveloped the whole country and determined the development of art and architecture.

From the sixth century BC onwards the region of Bihar was in real religious and philosophical ferment and most of the wandering philosophers seeking new paths to reach truth were active in Bihar. The natural resources particularly iron found in Bihar put it at the head of great political and economic revolution. The development of iron technology leading to possibility of large scale cultivation, construction of wide and long road-ways and expansion of trade and commerce released new forces in social and economic spheres which could not find legitimate scope in priest-dominated animal sacrifice (mostly cattle) oriented Brāhmanism. Religious discontent and socio- economic changes created the ideal condition for movement of religious reforms; and fertilized by the introduction of diverse racial and cultural tradition, the soil of Bihar proved most opportune.

Bihar in which Siddhārtha Gautama (567 BC - 487 BC) the Śākya prince of Kapilvastu, attained the supreme Enlightenment at Bodh-Gayā (532 BC), played an important part in the carrer of the Buddha and the history of Buddhism. It was in Bihar from Bodh-Gayā and Rājagṛha to Vaiśālī, along with other adjoining areas, where he spent forty five years preaching his cult and laying foundation of a strong church. Many rules and regulations were formulated here. The Nun's order was founded here at Vaiśālī. Many persons including the two chief disciples viz. Sariputra and Mahā Mogglana and Ambapālī of Vaiśālī accepted Buddhism and did much for it.

The itinerary of Siddhārtha or Gautama, the Buddha concerns the whole life of the great teacher; from time of his *Mahābhiniskramana* till his *Mahāparinirvāna* the Tathāgata sojourned in this region for most part of his life. After leaving Kapilvastu, Siddhārtha is said to have crossed the Acirāvati and from there he came to the āśrama of Ārāda kālāma via Kośala Pradeśa. From the āśrama of Ārāda kālāma via Kośala Pradeśa Gautama went to the āśrama of Uddakā Rāmaputra[1]. It is said that before coming to Rājagṛha, Gautama has first gone to these heretics where he was not satisfied with their philosophical approach. These two āśramas of Ārāda Kālāma and Uddakā Rāmaputra were certainly in Bihar[2]. According to *Lalitavistara,* the āśramas of Ārāda Kālāma and Udakā Rāmaputra were somewhere near Vaiśālī[3]. These places are said to have been located in between Bodha Gayā and Rājgir.[4] But D.D. Kosambi locates these places somewhere in Kośala Pradeśa.[5] The *Anguttara Nikāya* mentions Kesaputta Nigama as the name of the city of the Kālāma Kshatriyas H. Tripathi rightly concludes that the Keśaputta, with which the āśrama of Ārāda Kālāma has been identified by Kosambi was in the district of Shahabad in Bihar and not in Kośala Pradeśa. The present village of Keśatha is ancient Kesaputta of Buddhist India. Tripathi argues that the important branches of Kālāma Kshatriyas are still the inhabitants of Keśatha and an ancient temple of the village reflects the reminiscence of the past and hence these characteristics testify to the ancient character of the Kesatha village; Hoey has also located the āśrama of Ārāda Kālāma in the district of Shahabad, and has put forward arguments in favour of Ārāda to be Arrahs[6] name.

When Buddha's thirst for supreme knowledge could not be satisfied at the āśramas of Ārāda Kālāma and Uddakā Ramputra, he proceeded to Rājagṛha but here also the Tathāgata could not obtain the desired knowledge and finally left this place for Uruvilva (Urubela). Its neighbourhood was very much liked by Siddhārtha. It was here at Bodh-Gayā under the shade of famous Bodhi tree that Siddhārtha attained enlightenment[7] and came to be known as the Buddha. Rājagṛha[8] has been identified with present Rājgir and Uruvilva with Bodh-Gayā.[9]

After becoming the Buddha, he travelled and sojourned mostly within the boundary of Bihar.[10] As it has been stated earlier the Tathāgata passed about forty six years of his career as teacher at different places, mostly in Bihar and very few outside of it.[11] During these forty six years the Great Teacher stayed for a period of four months during the rainy season of every year at certain fixed place and for the remaining eight months of the year he devoted in preaching His faith by journeying from place to place. The following were the places of his sojourn during rains in chronological order.[12]

First rainy season at Rshipattana (Sārnāth)

Second to Fourth	,,	,,	Rajagṛha
Fifth	,,	,,	Vaiśālī
Sixth	,,	,,	Maṅkula Parvata

Seventh	,,	,,	Trayastriṁśa
Eight	,,	,,	Sumsumāragiri (Bharga)
Ninth	,,	,,	Kauśāmbī
Tenth	,,	,,	Pārileyaka
Eleventh	,,	,,	Nālāgrāma Magadha
Twelfth	,,	,,	Varianjā
Thirteenth	,,	,,	Cālīya Parvate
Fourteenth	,,	,,	Śrāvastī
Fifteenth	,,	,,	Kapilavastu
Sixteenth	,,	,,	Ālāvi
Seventeenth	,,	,,	Rājagṛha
Eighteenth to Nineteenth	,,	,,	Aṅga
Twentieth	,,	,,	Rājagṛha
Twentyfirst to Fortyfifth	,,	,,	Śrāvastī
Last of Fortysixth	,,	,,	Vališāī[13]

After the attainment of enlightenment the Buddha went directly to Sārnāth. And after the *Dharmacakrapravartana* he came to the city of Rājagṛha where he was extended standing ovation in the city of Bihar. This can be attested to by the fact that two hundred fifty disciples of Sanjay went alongwith Śāriputra and Maudgalyāyana to him and embraced his faith.

While the Buddha was sojourning at Rājagṛha, Caṇda Pradyota of Avanti sent his priest Mahākātyāna to request the Tathāgata to grace the kingdom of Avanti with His footprints, but the priest himself embraced the faith of the Buddha and was admitted to his Saṁgha.[14] It was at Rājagṛha that the Buddha had forbidden his disciples to exhibit any *radhi-prātihārya.*

In the third year of his ascetic career the Buddha, while so journing at Rājagṛha, went to Kapilvastu and initiated Rāhula. From Kapilvastu came to Vaiśāli and stayed there at the Kutagarāśālā. It was at Vaiśāli that the Mahāśramaṇa had initiated her aunt Mahāprajāpati Gautamī along with other five hundred women to the Saṁgha.[15]

It was at Rājagṛha during his fourth rainy season that the Buddha commanded the Bhiksus neither to sing nor to hear any song.

Once the Buddha along with five hundred disciples came to Nālandā and stayed at the Āmravana of a Śresthi called Prāvārika[16] at a time when Magadha was confronting a great famine. Nālandā has been identified with the village of Bargaon, seven miles to the north-west of Rājgir.[17] In the same year the Buddha went to Pañcaśālā, Magadhan village of Brāhmins, from where he returned with empty begging bowl.[18] It is difficult to locate this site.

In his eleventh rainy season the Buddha sojourned at Magadhan village, called Ekanālā, of Dakshinagiri.[19] Ekanālā has not yet been identified for want of other details.[20]

When the Buddha came from Vārānāsī and graced Vaiśālī for the second time, Sudinna, a young bachelor of the neighbouring village of Kalandaka requested the preaching Buddha to get himself initiated into Buddhism. The Buddha asked him to obtain the permission of his parents. Sundinna was admitted to the Saṁgha after he obtained his parent's permission. Later on, after ups and down in his ascetic career, Sudinna, along with his wife, attained Arhatship.[21] The Buddha came to Vaiśālī next and converted Simha Senāpati who was a follower of jainism. But the Tathāgata advised Simha Senāpati not to discontinue donations to the jains.[22]

The Great Teacher, during his sojourn at the Kūtāgāraśālā of Vaiśāī, won over Mahali, an important Vaiśālian and a great follower of Pūraṇā-Kāśyapa.[23] The Tathāgata is said to have gone to see a mendicant named Puṇḍarīka who lived somewhere in the neighbourhood of Vaiśālī. Puṇḍarīka was opposed to the faith of Ājīvikās but he was impressed by the Buddha.[24] In the very Kuṭāgāraśāla Sunakshartra Licchavi Youngman, was initiated and he lived with the Buddha as his personal servant (upasthapaka) for some time though later on he was turned out of the Saṁgha on account of his misconduct.[25]

The Buddha came from Vaiśālī to Bhaddiyā; twelve hundred and fifty Bhikshus accompanied the Great Teacher to that place. Bhaddiyā has been identified with the village of Bhadariya near Bhagalpur in the district of Bhagalpur.[26] The Tathāgata sojourned at jātivana of the locality where the entire family of Maṇḍaka was initiated into the church.[27] The Tathāgata reached guild of Āpana and sojourned there for some time. Āpana was a guild in the Aṅguttarāpa which has been identified with the district of Saharsa including the northern part of the district of Bhagalpur. Āpana may be located within the boundaries of the villages of Banagaon and Mahisi.[28]

The Great Teacher passed his thirteenth rainy season on the Cālity mountain, which is said to have been situated somewhere in Anga i.e. in the districts of Bhagalpur and Munger.[29]

According to the *Dīgha Nikāya* the Buddha is said to have sojourned at the village of Khāṇumata of Magadha; but it does not mention fromwhere the Great Teacher came to this place. The Buddha caryā records that the Tathāgata came here from Srāvastī but it is very difficult to locate Khāṇumata in the region of Magadha.[30] Here the Great Teacher had taught Kūṭadanta a Brāhmiṇ, learned in the Vedas, how to perform the yajña having sixteen parishkaras (ritualistic equipment) but violence.[31]

The Dīgha Nikāya records that the Buddha while sojouring in the country of Aṅga, had been to Gargarā Pushkarini of Champā,[32] but according to the Buddhacaryā the Great Teacher left Aṅga and came to Champā where he stayed on the bank of the Gargarā Pushkarini.[33] Champā has been identified with Champā nagar, situated at a distance of four miles to the west of Bhagalpur.[34] At the Gargarā-Pushkariṇi the Buddha had impressed Soṇadaṇḍa, the Brāhmaṇa lord of Champā, in an intellectual discussion, as a result of which the later became the follower of the former.[35] The Cullavagga mentions the Great Teacher to Kītāgiri from Śrāvastī.[36] Kītāgiri is situated in the kingdom of Kāśī.[37] Thereafter He came to Ālavī where He passed the sixteenth rainy season.[38] Rāhul Sankrityayana has identified Ālavī with Arwal falling by the side of road between Kanpur and Kannauj.[39] Differing from him H. Tripathi identified the present town of Arrah with ancient Ālavī, Tripathi further argues that while proceeding towards Kāśī and Rājagṛha, the Buddha came to Ālavi, hence Arwal of Kannauj cannot be Alavi of the Buddha.[40] Unfortunately Sita Ram Rai while discussing the itinerary of the Buddha in Bihar has failed to give the exact location of Ālavī which still remains a riddle. From Ālavī the Buddha came to Rājagṛha where He stayed at Kalandakanivāpa of Venubana.[41] The Tathāgata spent his seventeenth rainy season. But the circumstances were unfavourable because Rājagṛha was famine stricken. One of the important declarations by the Buddha was that Maitrāyaniputra was the best of all Śramaṇas.[42]

The Buddha passed his eighteenth and nineteenth rainy seasons on the Cāliya mountain in Aṅga. During this period of two years the Mahāśramaṇa extensively toured the different parts of eastern Bihar and had religious discourses with many house holders and Brāhmaṇas.[43] The Buddha left Aśvapura for Kanjangala and having reached there He sojourned in its

Venuvana.[44] Kanjangala has been identified with the present Santhal Parganas.[45]

The Buddha went from Krnatangala to Suhma[46] and from there to the region of Setakaṇṇika.[47] Suhma was somewhere betweenVaṅga and Kaliṇga, [48] and Setakaṇṇika was none but the region of Hazaribagh, where the mica is found in abundance, for 'Setakaṇṇika' means the region of mica.

The Buddha again returned to the Cāliya mountain in order to pass His nineteenth rainy season.

From here He proceeded to Śrāvasti but came to Rajagṝha to pass his twentieth rainy season. During this trip to Rājagṛha the Great Teacher went to Dakṣiṇagiri. The Tathāgata again returned to Rājagṝha and stayed on the Gṛdhrakūṭa mountain. The sojourn of the Buddha on the Gṛdhrakūṭa mountain was important because king Bimbisāra had invited all the village headmen of his kingdom, numbering about eighty thousands to hear the discourse by the Great Master. But to their surprise the Tathāgata asked his personal attendant Swagat to show miracles by flying in the sky. The later obeyed the Mahāśramaṇa and as a result all people present there became followers of Buddha. After staying for a considerable period at Rājgṝha, the Great Teacher proceeded again towards Vaiśālī. This time also the Buddha stayed at Kūṭāgārśālā of Mahāvana. Now the Great Teacher was fifty-five years old.

According to *Aṅguttara Nikāya* the Buddha is said to have passed his succeeding twenty-five rainy seasons (from the twenty-first to the forty-fifth) at Śrāvastī alone. But the Great Teacher continued his tour to different places including those of Bihar.

Once the Buddha came to the region of Mithilā named Makhādevāmravana.[49] Here He succeeded in converting an old Brāhmaṇa named Brahmāyu.[50] The Great Teacher, while touring in the region of Kośala came to Keśaputta which has been rightly identified with the village of Kesath, about five miles to the south of Dumraon in the district of Sahabad.[51] The Buddha delivered some of His sermons to the local Kālāma kshatriyas.

Once upon a time, after sojouring at Kośāmbī, came to Rājagṛha where he had to face many troubles created by Devadatta, but the latter was everywhere shown down.

Once the Buddha has gone out of Rājagṛha. When He was returning it was evening. He stayed in the house of a potter named Bhārgava. Here he met Pushkarasāti Dedana Brāhmaṇa, ruler of Taxila, who had come in search of the Great Teacher for the purpose of being initiated into His faith.[52] The Buddha, while touring, went to Nālandā and stayed at his old Prāvārika mango-grove. Here, Upāli, a famous house holder of Nālandā was converted.[53] The Buddha again returned to Rājagṛha and stayed in the mango-grove of Jīvaka. Here he saved Cullatpanthak, a disappointed Bhiksu from renouncing the Monkhood. When the Buddha came to Rājagṛha next time he was with one thousand two hundred and fifty Bhikṣus. This time also he stayed in mango-grove of Jīvaka. During this trip He delivered sermon to Ajātaśatru. But he was not much impressed.[54]

The Buddha then went to Śrāvastī where He erected a Chaitya upon the corporeal relics of Śāriputra. When he was in Vajji on way to Rājagṛha, the death of Maudgalyāyana was communicated to Him. Deeply shocked he came to Rājagṛha and erected a Chaitya on the corporeal relics of Maudgalyāyana.

The Buddha is sojourning in a Maghadhan village, named Mātula after the nirvāṇa of Sāriputra and Maudgalyāyana. It was here that the Māhāśramaṇa had asked the Bhikṣus to be self dependent as far as practicable.

The Buddha left Gṛdhrakūṭa and proceeded towardsNālandā. He stopped in the way near Ambalatthikā where he stayed at Rājāgāraka for the night. Ambalatthikā has been identified with present Silao lying between Rājagṛha and Nālandā.[55] Here the Buddha has preached the *Brahmajālasutta* to the Bhikṣus.

The Buddha came from Nālandā to Pāṭaliputra when Vassākāra and Sunitha two ministers of Ajātaśatru were engaged in fortifying the city of Pāṭaliputra. The Tathāgata with His party stayed at the royal guest-house of the city.[56] The Great Teacher crossed the Ganga and reached Ukkācela. The gate of the city from which the Buddha passed and the ghāta from where he crossed the river were called after His name the Gautama. Gate may be identified with the spot near Gurudvārā in Patna City and the Gautama ghāta may have been the present Gāya ghāta.[57] Ukkacela has been identified by Rahul Sankrityayana with the present Hajipur.[58]

The Great Teacher left Ukkācela for Koṭigrāma and proceeded from there to Nadikā. He sojourned there at Ginjakavasatha,[59] where He had already sojourned in the past.[60] Kotigrāma[61] may have been near Hajipur and Nadikāgrāma may be identified with the present Lalganj both lying between Hajipur and Vaiśāli. At Nadikā the Buddha had met His three disciples Aniruddha, Nandiya and Kimbila. This meeting of the Buddha with these three Bhiksus was praised by a yaksa who said that it was due to the good luck of the region of Vajji that the Buddha and his disciples graced that land.

The Buddha then went to Vaiśālī, but this time He did not go to Kūṭāgāraśālā of the place. He stayed at the mango-grove of Āmrapāli, the famous courtesan of Vaiśālī. It is believed that the Buddha had passed his last rainy season at *veluvagrāma* of Vaiśālī. This was his last visit to the region of Vaiśālī because he died before the commencement of forty-sixty rainy season. When the Tathāgata was better in health He moved to Kūṭāgāraśālā of Mahāvana where he foretold that he would attain *Mahāparinirvāṇa* after three months. The last sojourn of the Mahāśramaṇa in the land of Bihar was at Bhoganagara which was according to Rahul Sankrityayana somewhere in the district of Saran or in the western most limit of the district of Muzzaffarpur.[62] After the forgoing discussion it becomes perfectly clear that the Buddha extensively toured not only northern Bihar but also major part of the sourthern Bihar for popularising his cult. It was a result of his painstaking and strenuous journey in Bihar that the faith of Lord Buddha was grounded on a solid footing. Bihar has the biggest role in contributing to the spread of Buddhism. The last year (488-487 B.C.) of the physical life of the Lord was spent in Bihar. After his *Mahāparinirvāṇa* at Kusinagar (UP) the remains of his body divided into eight shares and distributed among the different parties that had staked their claims for them including some from like the republican Licchavi of Vaiśālī, and the monarchical Ajātśatru of Rājagṛha.

The history of Buddhism in the next and a helf century shows that the first three Buddhist councils were held on the soil of Bihar, at Rājagṛha, Vaiśālī and Pāṭaliputra in the reign periods of Ajātśatru, Aśoka the black (Kālā Aśoka) and Aśoka Maurya respectively where the Buddhist canons were reduced to writing. The three *piṭakās* as we find them took almost the present shape about the time of emperor Aśoka, the Maurya in the third Century BC. That the first three successive Buddhist councils were held in Bihar speaks of the importance given to this land. These councils played a prominent role in shaping the ideas and in the spread of this cult. This aforesaid fact clearlydemonstrates that Bihar was the land of hectic activities and as it has been said the first three Buddhist councils were held here. By the time we reach Aśoka (269-232 BC), we find that a local cult has been completely transformed into an all India religion and is heading towards having an important place in the world. It has its own school of art and architecture through the Buddha relics, stūpas, Chaityas, Vihāras, Pillars, Rock engravings and cave-dwellings. It may now be safely concluded that Bihar was the cradle of Buddism and it was here that

Buddism, as a movement came to occupy a place of great importance in the world history.

It is unfortunate that the history of the development of Buddhism in Bihar, which was not only its birth place but also a centre for laying its solid foundation leading to its dissemination throughout the world; has not engaged attention of the scholars proportionate to its value. The period from the rise of Buddism to the end of the third century AD is very important because there are many ups and downs in the history of Buddhism during this period. It is, therefore, desirable that there should be a separate and independent work on the history of Buddhism in Bihar. The title "Buddhism in Bihar" (from the Sixth century BC to the third century AD) appears to be justified because so far there has been no independent work on Buddhism in Bihar. The one entitled *Baudha dharma aur Bihar* by Hawaldar Tripathi is neither exhaustive nor it deals with the development of Buddhism and the branching of it into many sects and sub-sects.

The comprehensive history of Bihar edited by B.P. Sinha is another work on the history of Bihar but this also does not deal with the histroy of Buddhism in Bihar in detail. It fails to elaborate how Buddism which was a local cult in the beginning culminated into a strong peoples' movemnt which compelled or inspired many kings to adopt as their personal religion and also as the state religion. The present work is, therefore, a need of the hour. The thesis is an humble attempt to trace the history of the development of Buddism. The data gathered from the literary sources have been corroborated with the help of archaeological sources as far as possible. It is not claimed that the work is entirely original one but it no doubt succeeds in presenting a compact, vivid account of the history of development of the Buddhism in Bihar. This in itself is no mean contribution to the advancement of knowledge on the subject.

This work consists of the following chapter besides an introduction in the beginning and a conclusion at the end.

(1) *Origin and early spread of Buddhism* (up to the coronation of Aśoka in 269 BC). (2) *Beginnings of Buddhist Art in the pre-Aśokan period* (532 BC - 269 BC). (3) *Development of Buddhism in the time of Aśoka and the later Mauryas* (269 B.C. - 188 BC). (4) *Condition of Buddhism in the period between the fall of the Mauryas and the rise of the Kanishka group of Kushana kings,* (188 BC-AD 78). (5) *Transformation of Buddhism from the time of Kanishka to the end of the third century AD.*

REFERENCE

1. Majjhima Nikāya, 2, 4, 5; Narendra Deva, Bauddha-dharma darśana; p. 4.
2. *CHB;* Vol. 1, part 1, p. 927.
3. *Ibid.*
4. Rahul Sankrityayana, *Buddha-Caryā;* 1988 V.S.
5. D.D. Kosambi, *Bhagavana Buddha,* p. 116.
6. *JASB,* Vol. LXIX, p. 77.
7. H. Tripathi, *Buddha-dharma aur Bihar,* pp. 43-45; Suttanipata, 27; H. oldenburg, *Buddha;* p. 105-112.
8. N.L. Dey, *Geographical Dictionary of Ancient and Medieval India;* (1927), p. 165.
9. *Ibid;* p. 212.
10. The boundary of Bihar means the present limits of the State of Bihar.
11. *Anguttara Nikaya;* 2, 3, 5, Rahul Sankrityayana, op. cit., p. 75.
12. *Ibid;* p. 75.

13. H. Tripathi opines that the Buddha after enlightenment passed only forty-five rainy seasons, for he left home at the age of twentynine, attained enlightenment at the age of thirtyfive and died at the age of eighty on the full moon day of the month of Vaiśākha, certainly before the commencement of the rainy season, H. Tripathi op. cit., p. 77.
14. *Aṅguttara Nikāya* (Atthakatha); i. 1,10.
15. *Ibid;* XVIII, 2,1-3; the identification of Vaiśālī may be seen in the itinerary of Chinese pilgrims.
16. *Samyutta Nikāya;* VL, 9.
17. N.L. Dey, *op. cit;* pp. 136-37.
18. *Samyutta Nikāya;* iv, 2, 8.
19. *Anguttara Nikāya;* iv, 2, 8.
20. N.L. Dey, op.*cit;* p. 51.
21. *Buddha-Cārya;* p. 145; *Cullavaggo;* XI, 1, 2; *Vinaya Pitaka;* 1.
22. *Buddha-Cāryā;* p. 14.
23. *Dīgha Nikāya* (Mahalisutta) 1, 6.
24. *Majjhima Nikāya;* III, 1, 5.
25. *Ibid,* III, 1, 5.
26. H. Tripathi, *op. cit.,* p. 89.
27. *Mahāvaggo;* vi, 5, 1, 1.
28. H. Tipathi, *op. cit.,* p. 90.
29. H. Tipathi, *op. cit.,* p. 93.
30. *Rahul Sankrityayana :* Buddha Caryā; *p. 232.*
31. *Digha Nikāya; i.* 5.
32. *Ibid;* i, 4.
33. Rahul Sankrityayana, *Buddha-Caryā;* p. 241.
34. N.L. Dey, *op. cit;* p. 44.
35. *Dīgha Nikāya* (Soṇadaṇḍasuta); i, 4.
36. *Cullavagga;* vi, 5, 2.
37. *Majjhima Nikāya;* iii, 2, 10 .

38. *Cullavagga; vi*, 5, 4.
39. Rahul Sankrityayana,*Vinayapitaka;* p. 472.
40. H. Tripathi, *op. cit.*, p. 97.
41. *Cullavagga; vi*, 5, 4.
42. Majjhima Nikāya; *i, 3, 4.*
43. CHB; *Vol. I, part I, p. 938.*
44. Aṅguttara Nikāya; *i, 1, 3, 8.*
45. Rahul Sankrityayana, *Buddha-Caryā*; p. 289.
46. *Aṅguttara Nikaya*: iv. 3, 1.
47. *Samyutta Nikāya*; xiv, 3, 10.
48. N. L. Dey, *op. cit.* p. 195.
49. Majjhima Nikāya; *ii, 4, 3.*
50. *Ibid;* ii, 5, 1.
51. H. Tripathi, *op., cit.*, p. 120.
52. *Majjhima Nikāya;* iii, 4, 10.
53. *Ibid;* ii, 1, 6.
54. *Dīgha* Nikāya; i, 2.
55. *H. Tripathi,* op. cit., *p. 129*.
56. *Dīgha Nikāya;* ii, 3.
57. H. Tripathi, *op. cit.*, p. 130.
58. Rahul Sandrityayana, *Buddha-Caryā*; p. 529.
59. *Digha Nikāya;* II 3, 2.
60. *Majjhima Nikāya*; v, 4, 1.
61. Y. Mishra, *Homage to Vaiśālī;* pp. 149-50.
62. Rahul Sankrityayana, Sāhitya-kāra (Buddhāṅaka); Sahitya kara Sansad, Allahabad, 1956.

Chapter II

Origin and Early Spread of Buddhism

(Up to the coronation of Aśoka in 269 BC)

Buddhism arose and flourshed in eastern Uttar Pradesh and Bihar, in the kingdoms of Magadha and Kosala. The Buddha spent most of his time in Bihar and after his death three councils were held successively at Rāgjaha, Vaiśālī and Patliputra. Why is it that north eastern India became the cradle of Buddhism in the sixthfourthcenturies BC ? Did the heterodox sects arise merely as a reaction to the ritual ridden religion of the Vedic people? The real key to the understanding of the rise of new religious movement lies in certain significant development in the material life of the people.

Before going into the factors responsible for the origin and spread of Buddhism, one must attempt to explore the socio-political conditions what made the development of Buddhism inevitable in Bihar. Once this newly founded religion saw its origin, it spread at a very fast note. Buddha preached the gospel of 'non-violence' Which was against the basic tenets of Vedic cult. The Vedas involved several Yajñas which resulted in the killings of animals on a large scale. On the other hand, Brāhmānas were the profiteers in these killings. The Vedas had given special privileges to the priestly class in the society.

Contrary to it, Lord Buddha renounced violence and in other way questioned the supremacy of the Brāhmāṇas in the society. It was quite natural that the Buddha's idea of non-violence alienated that section of the society who had unquestioned hold over the social laws.

The rise of Buddhism took place at an epoch when not only India but also Greece, Persia and China were experiencing a stir in religious matter through the advent of Socrates with his distinguished pupils and contemporary philsophers in Greece, of Zoroaster in Persia, and of Lao-tse and Confucius in China.

The sacrifices were believed, if rightly performed, to secure for them wealth, health, long life and strength, the good will and good grace of the gods in this world, and happiness in the other world. But the dubious among them began to question within themselves whether there was not the chance of this belief being wrongly based. Side by side with the elaborate sacrifices performed by the house holders, there were prescribed shortened forms of them, or even mere cognition of the supreme, unaccompanied with any rituals for the *vānaprasthas* and the Yatis. Similar views more or less developed and opposed to the *Karma Kāṇḍa* of the Brāhmāṇas and specially to the cruel slaying of animals in the sacrifices, were already in the air before Buddha arose to preach his doctrines.[1] Brāhmanism allowed various shades of philosophic and religious views to grow up within its fold without taking objection to their existence within its limits. But the key to the reception of this toleration lay in the fact that the dissenting view, side by side with its opposition to one more Brāhmānic doctrines, showed its allegiance to one or more of the ultimate fundamental tenets of Brāhmanism such as the affiliation to the Vedas, belief in their authority, worship of any of the Brāhmanic gods as such, recognition of the authority of the Brāhmāṇas, or compliance with the caste-system[2]. It is only when we keep this in view that we can understand how the sects like *vedānta* or *Sānkhya* could hold to their doctrines and yet continue to be recognized by the

Brāhmaṅas as orthodox. The elasticity of Brāhmanism was, no doubt, a source of its strength, and the existence of this toleration was the cause by which Brāhmanism could grow into a ramified religion, as wide as the India continent. But there was a limit to the degree to which the heresy of its views could be carried by a Brahmanic sect as such. This limit was crossed by the Buddha, who stood up as a rock to stop the flow of the religion in order to direct the faiths of the people. He preached that religious truths lay, not in the sacrifices, not in the Vedas which prescribed these sacrifices, not in the worship of many deities of the Brāhmanic pantheon, not in the observance of the caste-rules, not in the magical practices of the *Atharva veda,* not in the extreme forms of self-mortifications, and not, in short, in the many other pet beliefs and practices that came as corollaries to an allegiance to the bases of Brāhmaṇic faiths, but in self-culture 'culminating in Arhatship' which constitutes the key-stone of Buddhism.[3]

Buddha's view against sacrifices and the rites or acts involved in them have been expressed in no uncertain terms throughout his sayings. Against the memorising of the vedic mantra and their fruitless repetitions to retain them in memory, he tauntingly remarked that the Brāhmāṅas were nothing but the repeaters of the hymns composed by the ancient sages such as *Ahaka, Vāmka,* Vāmadeva, Vessamitta, etc.[4] He also disparaged the sacrifices involving needless expenses and payments of heavy fees[5] to *Brāhmāṇas* who, by dint of their craftiness, made them the means of procuring wealth for themselves.[6] The rituals were meaningless operations so minutely but mehanically compiled by the sarcificing Brāhmāṇas[7], intending to keep their superstitious clients under a perpetual and unquestioning tutelage. In the pāyāsisuttanta,[8] Kumāra kassapa, an immediate disciple of Buddha instructs prince Pāyāsi that the celebration of sacrifices without curelty involved in the killing of victims is a degree better than the celebration thereof accompanied with the perpetration of that curelty. A similar view is expressed by Buddha in the *kūṭadanta sutta,*[9] where mention is made of sects or rituals to which toleration can be shown in the ascending order in which they are arranged; sacrifice in which living creatures are slaughtered; better than this is the one performed with only ghee, oil, butter, honey and sugar; better still than this is charity, specially that extended to holy men; better than this again is the building of monasteries; and better than this is the observance of moral precepts; and the best of all is the 'sacrifice' of the four-fold meditation.[10] In short, Buddha condemns the sacrifices in a general way referring to them as but a 'low art' unworthy of whatever a Brāhmāṇa should be according to his conception.[11] The Buddhist rejection of animal sacrifice and emphasis on non-injury to animals assumed a new significance in the context of needs of new agriculture. A joint protest against sacrifice is found in some later vedic references. In the Rig-veda the term *aghanya* or not to be killed is mostly used for a milk giving cow and it generally occurs in later portion of the text.[12] The same term is also used for cattle at several places in the Atharva-veda[13] which also gives considerable evidence of agriculture but numerous references to cattle sacrifice suggest that normally the killing of animal including numerous cattle was approved of by the Vedic ideology. In sharp contrast to this Gautama, the Buddha asserts that animal sacrifice does not produce any merit. He favours a Yajña which does not involve sacrifice. We have the story of a rich Brāhmāna called *Uggata Sarira* who collected numerous animals for sacrifice but at the advice of Buddha released them. This Brāhmāṇa was asked to raise sacrificial fire for the sake of parents, for wife, children, servants and retainers and for holy men and recluses.[14]

Gautama Buddha pointedly and specifically attacked Vedic sacrifices in which animals were killed. It is said that once when he was visiting Śrāvastī, Prasenjit, the king of Koisala started a great sacrifice in which 500 oxen, 500 male calves,

500 female calves and 500 sheeps were tied to the sacrificial post.[15] The slaves and messengers of the king threatened by fear and force, were making preparations for this sacrifice with tears in their eyes.[16] When this was reported to the Master, he remarked that the *Aśvamedha, Puruṣmedha* and *Vājpeya* etc. did not produce good results. Sages of good conduct did not prescribe those sacrifices in which various beings such as goat, sheep and cattle were killed.[17] Great sages of good conduct recommended those sacrifices in which goat, sheep and cattle were not killed.[18]

For the first time in India histroy did a single individual venture to speak emphatically against all that was dear to the leaders of the then Brāhmāṇic society with their numerous to help them and with the combined belief of almost the whole population of India to support them;[19] and for the first time also did an Indian undertake to support his view by practically remoulding the existing social element into an organization that could successfully stamp out or keep in abeyance the opposed ideas and practices in India for several centuries and are even now materialising the wishes of the great Reformer to a great exent in a few localities in India and in a few countries outside India.[20]

It was this doctrine of *ahiṁsā* that appealed so much to the hearts of the people. Mahāvira also launched upon the field of Indian thought before Buddha which is doctrine of ahiṁsā but his followers carried it to such an excess that it could not draw the admiration of the Brāhmāṅas while the rational view of same taken by Buddha attracted the attention of every one, no mattter, whatever creed he might profess. Every body knows that owing to the radical doctrines that Buddha preached, there was no love lost between the Brāhmāṇas and the Buddhists, and yet the inclusion of Buddha as an *avātara* is no doubt a clear testimony of the infinite kindnesss with which Buddha's heart was imbued to which even his enemies had to pay homage by including him in their pantheon.

The doctrine of ahimsā was but an off shoot of the *mettā* feeling which embraced not merely the negative restraint upon causing pain to any living creatures but also positive acts of charity and love, removing or attempting to remove distress, wherever existing and whatever form they might assume. Standing on this catholic view-point, the outlook of the Buddhists on caste-restrictions that introduced differences in degrees of high and low were accompanied in many instances with narrowness and hatred obstructing the exercise of *mettābhāva*, could not but be as it was enunciated by Buddha. Buddha has on many occasions asked his disciples to exercise the *mettā* feeling as one of the methods of attaining perfection in *samādhi* and alongwith it the kindered feelings of *kāruṇa* (compassion), *muditā* (sympathy in other Joy), and *Uperkkhā* (equanimity).[21]

Many of the historians still tend to believe that Buddha restricted his preachings to the religious level only but it is far from true. Buddha was more a social reformer than a religious leader. It is true that he concentrated his ideas on religious matters but he at the sametime led a *potent drive* against social rigidity. He included women and śudras in his *saṁgha*, though he did not attack caste rigidity in its extreme form as the jainas did. Buddha moderately attacked it and tolerated it not due to fear of opposition from the Brāhmāṇas but to save the society from great unheavals. Buddha's eight fold path lays great stress on social problems rather than religions. 'Ahiṃsā' itlelf had social and economic relevance. The brahmanic tradition of sacrifices did often result in the slaughter of animals which in one way or other harmed agrarian situation. The call for check on such slaughter gave necessary respite to those who involved themselves in production.[22]

The Brāhmanic standpoint had its basis in birth and in the cosmology by which the four castes were given the order of precedence of the limbs of the great puruṣa supposed to have existed at the time of the creation of the universe.[23] Buddha on the other hand took a rational view of the subject and wanted the individuals to be higher and lower according to their respective qualities and not according to the accident of birth;[24] and instead of the cosmology looked upon by him as erroneous, he pointed to a cosmology of his own described in the Aggañña *suttānta*[25] and representing according to him the real state of things. He mentions in a descending scale beginning from the gods with their higher qualities and ending with men who possessed much inferior qualities and among the latter were classes formed according to avocations and the members of these classes could easily transfer themselves from one to another by developing the qualities for the avocations of the class to which they transferred themselves. In connection with his replies to questions[26] and the discussions to which they led Buddha has given hints showing that the kṣatriyas could be superior to the Brāhmāṇas, if by qualities the former were in reality superior to the latter; for the element of birth which was set out as the criterion of status by the Brāhmāṅas was in fact a thing which reason cannot support. It could not be denied that there were Brāhmāṇas who though claiming to be the highest in social status by their birth were inferior to many a member of the lowest caste by their habits and inferior qualities. Buddha pointed this out as a very unreasonable disposition of social element to put those higher who by nature were lower. As regards monastic life, there could never be any distinction, exception that brought about by stages of moral and spiritual progress on the path towards arhathood. As rivers lose their identity after merging in the ocean waters, similarly an individual loses his identity after joining the monastic order.[27] It should be observed that Buddh'a attitude in regard to castes is an expression of the feeling of brother-hood that he wanted to prevail among all beings. When we look at the matter from this standpoint, we see that this attitude was but a logical extension of his view of relations among human beings.

It was thus that Buddha held views subversive of the sacrifices and the caste-system, the two main bases of the then existing

Brahmaṇism. With such views of the two bases of Brāhmaṇism he could not naturally keep terms with the Brāhmṇa as in the acceptance of the authority of the Vedas.

In the SILUVIMAMSA *Jatāka*[28] the Boddhisattta says, "of no value are the Vedas, of no value is birth or *kinsman* for the future world; only one's own pure virtue brings him happiness in the next world". Buddha disbelieves the revealed character of the Vedas by remarking that the ancient sages *Atṭhaka. Vāmaka, Vāmadeva, Vāssamitta,* etc. never saw Brahman from whom they state to have received the vedic texts.[29]

'Many times in the history of religions has the protestant having thus carried the outer defences of an orthodox faith, believed that there remained no other citadel. It may be, on the other hand, that Gautama knew of the existence of such a Brāhmān citadel where truth was held. At first sight nothing can appear more definite than the opposition of the Buddhist *An-attā, no-Atmān,* and the Brāhmān Atman-the sole reality. It is frankly admitted by Rhys. Davids that,

"The neuter-Brahman is, so far as I am aware, entirely unkown in the Nikāyas, and of course the Buddha's idea of Brāhman, in the masculine, really differs widely from that of the up anisads."[30]

Worship of such divine beings was of no avail, for they were unable to raise men to a higher status by dint of their own powers; for it was man's own virtue that could elevate him morally and spiritually, and not any external help from the gods. Of this import is the following passage from the *Brahmajāla Suttānta*: "worship of sun, worship of the great one, invocation of *siri,* the goddess of luck, the vowing of gifts to a god for the grant of benefit, the offering of sacrifices to the gods are low arts from which Gautama, the recluse holds him aloof."[31] The attack of the *Mimāmsakas* upon the Buddhists on the ground that the latter themselves looked upon their texts as revealed proceeds upon the imputation of an idea to the original Buddhists they did not entertain.[32]

The Buddha discouraged the magical practices and the rites of the *Atharva Veda* and even the practice of other arts not excluding astrology, by which men were led to commit deviations from the right conduct. It is needless to say that many of these practices were of a puerile character such as performing rites for averting the supposed consequences of evil omens such as the sitting of a hawk on the roof of a house, etc. the magical rites are performed in the belief that the things desired by an individual can be procured by virtue of those rites as certainly as a particular effect follows a particular cause; and moreover, the belief in the efficacy of these rites inspires one with the idea that abnormal powers can be acquired through them so that right conduct which is believed to be productive of happiness or spiritual good might be discarded, and magical rites made to take its place. This idea is detrimental to the pursuit of virtue and this was perhaps one of the reasons why Buddha did not countenance these rites, apart from the question of superstitions underlying them.[33]

It is clear from the dissatisfaction expressed by the Buddha at the fruitlessness of his own mortifications during his spiritual discipleship under several preceptors in the first six years after his renunciation of the world that he lost his belief in the modifications as means to salvation.[34] His enlightenment was preceded by the pursuit of the middle path in which the use of the necessaries of life as to food was not regarded as an obstacle in the attainment of spiritual success. Just as on the one hand the use of these necessities must be combined with moral conduct and meditation, so on the other, the ascetic practices, if adopted in a moderate degree, must be associated with the same two essentials of spiritual life. Sanction was given by Buddha to a moderate use of ascetic practices as a concession[35] to the strong tendency of the Indian mind, imbued as it had been for a long time with the belief in the efficacy of such penances to resort to the extreme forms of abstinence from comforts of life or even painful methods of positively inflicting pain upon the body as aids to the acquisition of spiritual merit in the direction of the mind towards the spirtitual ideals. Buddha himself declared the hollowness of such extreme practices but left the moderate ones to be intertwined into the programme of life of the Buddhist monks who must in all cases look upon the observance of the moral precepts in the practice of meditation as forming essentially the basis of his religion. Suffice it to say that Buddha insisted on the moral purity in the use of speech, mind and body for all those who joined the Buddhist order in and through which the salvation lies. He prescribes certain rules for observance by the laity but the means to salvation does not exist in their ways of life though conforming to the prescribed rules. The means are to be found in the monastic order which for this reason engaged principally his attention. This is a great departure from the doctrines of the Brāhmāṅas whose śāstrās declare that salvation is not the monopoly of monastic or asceric life[36] but is equally within the reach of students or house holders provided they desire it keenly in and through the performance of their respective duties. As to the mode of meditation adopted by Buddha, it is evident from the Buddhist works or extracts on meditation. Such as the *Mahāsatep atthāna suttanta,* the *patisambhi damagga,* the *Visuddhimagga* etc. that it was kept from the practices belonging to Haṭhayoga as also from the several forms of *āssana* or *Praṅāyāma.* For instance in the Majjhima Nikāya,[37] Buddha inculcates the avoidance of the mechanical process by which the tongue is pushed backwards towards the palate, a device that is so often resorted to in the Hindu system of Yoga. Buddha has in short desired to keep his *Yogamārga* free from anything that is fanciful, severe of unnecessary to the concentration of the mind.[38] Moreover the abnormal devices need to create a pride in the minds of the sādhakas and impress the uninstructed spectators, if any, with admiration which might tempt the former to utilize it for worldly purposes.[39] The Buddhist path of meditation is thus a simplified process in which the elements of the Brāhmanic Yoga exist sometimes with slight modifications but which has been kept clear of what was looked upon as either unnecessary, extraneous or dangerous. It is suited to whoever joins the monastic order, provided by the exercise of *śīla,* he had succeeded in developing frames of body and mind in which he could launch himself on an attempt at concentration of mind leading to the ultimate wisdom. "The states (Samāpatti) in the Buddhist system of meditation were of importance, not merely of importance for learners as a means for arriving at Nirvāṇa, but the temporal release these afforded from the sense-precepts and the concrete was so highly esteemed that they were looked upon as luxuries and enjoyed as such by the saints and by the Buddha himself."[40] The ultimate object with which these meditations and forms of discipline were undertaken and towards which Buddha rose to lead the people in his easy but certain way was Nirvāṇa.

The significance of Nirvāṇa has assumed various complexions at the hands of interpreters but this much is certain that the attainment of same meant for an individual a *permanent escape from the whirling of karma and rebirth* with their attendant miseries. It is futile for us to try to define what is meant by this term: the Vedāntists might identify it with union with the *Brāhmān,* the indescribable substratum of the phenomenal universe, the votaries of any of the highest deities such as Sive or Viṣṇu might call it *mukti,* or the Christians might think it to be nothing but salvation as conceived by them; but the fact remains that the Buddha is himself absolutely silent as to what he wanted the term to really mean. This attitude of the Buddha is perhaps significant from one point of view namely his general unwillingness to enter onto ultimate questions of metaphysics; for a definition or a description of Nirvanā would certainly have led to the mention of things which would have proved a good ground for fruitless discussions among his followers as well as among the Buddhists and non-Buddhists. To those who are far away from the state in which Nirvāṇa is attained, the thing might be a subject of difference of opinion, but to those who attained it, was clear as a perception, though the attendant conceptions and feelings may lie beyond the power of language to express. Indeed disputes as to ontological questions often prove to be no better than quarrels over tweedledum and tweedledee. The Buddha was perfectly aware of the worthlessness of such discussions and their evil consequences and has for that reason been uniformly silent over questions which other wise might have given rise to undesirable results.[41] Suffice it to say that Buddhism relies ultimately upon success in Yoga without which the life of a Buddhist cannot be complete. This is the fruition to which Buddhism leads and for the attainment of which it proposes to show the shortest way.

It will thus be seen that Buddhism struck out a path, of which easiness and simplicity were the characteristic features.These two features depended upon the fact that the undue importance attached by the Hindus to rites and practices that were difficult to undertake on account of their elaborateness of expenses and the arduousness involved in them, was absent in Buddhism. There were other reasons also for which Buddhism could attract the people so far as its tenets and practices were concerned:

1. The avoidance of metaphysical questions rendered it easily intelligible to the masses.

2. The greater play of reason instead of belief that in the Brāhāmanic system is so pre-emptorily demanded by the sacred texts and in so wide a range of matters was an attractive feature to the people who developed more than other the habits of reasoning for themselves the good and bad side of the religious questions.

3. Buddhism appealed to the common masses on account of the doctrine of āhimsā coåntrary to vedic cult of sacrificing animals from which the Brāhmānas drew their sustenance. Buddhism advocated banning of slaughter due to the growing

need of animals for cultivation. The use of iron from the 8th century B.C. involved farming on a large scale than before and it could not have been done without animals. Sacrifices resulted in the shortage of animals retarding the processes of increased farming. Therefore, it became call of the time to preach ahimsā what Buddhism perfectly did.

The growing importance of farming and its resultant effect on productivity made vaiśyas aware of their rights in the society. Brāhmanic religion followed strict varṇa norms in which vaiśyas and śudras had no fair deal. They were oppressed and were restricted from enjoying freedom due to caste rigidity. It is also to be noted that as soon as the vaiśyas grew richer, naturally they would have sought a position in the society. In this regard, Buddhism provided much solace to them. It must be kept in view that vaiśyas were the only tax paying class and social tension along this line also existed in the society. Buddhism dis-favoured caste or varṇa rigidity.

4. Buddhism did not rely so much upon appeals to the supernatural as Brāhmaṅism did, always referring to their efficacy shown in unseen ways by the utterance of mantras, the performance of sacrifices, and in fact, compliance with many rituals prescribed in the śāstras. The reference to this unseen and supernatural element in Brāhmaṅism became so much exaggerated that an error in the smallest detail of a ritual or a mistake in the utterance of a single syllable of a mantra had to be expiated by proper ceremonies or rectified by going through the same things again, and the belief of the clients of the priests appears to have approved of such demands upon their credence. There are many other directions in which exaggerated demands upon the belief of the laity in general were made by the Brāhmaṅas. But Buddhism was shorn to a very great extent of such utilizations of the supernatural element that often

mystified the vision of the laity in regard to having a clear idea of what the religion was and what they were actually doing. This gave Buddhism a practical turn making it include rites and ceremonies with their accompanying formulas that the masses could understand and the reason of which was generally patent to their understanding.

5. The language in which it was preached and its ceremonies conducted was the dialect of the people concerned and therefore their reason could obtain greater scope for exercise in the intelligent following of the discourse or the rituals to which they attended, while Sanskrit used by the Brāhmaṅas in connection with all religious matters could not satisfy them in these respects.

6. The great stress laid by Buddhism upon right conduct, so much so that it became one of its most prominent features, was also an attractive factor. Buddhism is often described as an ethical religion on the ground of the prominence of this feature as against several others that are emphasised in other systems of religion. From the very time when a convert enters into the monastic order up to the time when he attains to *arhathood*, the keynote of his life is right conduct. Ordinarily the unsophisticated conscience of even an untutored man approves very greatly the intrinsic rightness of a scheme of conduct that proposes to deal our goodwill and charity to all, and demands strict *continence*, and silent forbearance that sees an error in an act where other would have seen offence and ill will. Upon this view of man that has its root in his inborn conscience rests the strength of the tables of the rules of conduct for general guidance like the ten commandments of the Bible and it was to this element in man's mental constitution that this side of Buddhism appealed so much, and appeals even now.

7. The prevalence of the practice of Yoga had become widely spread for a long time previous to the advent of Buddha and carried with it the general belief among the Hindus that it was one of the most potent instrument for effecting the highest spiritual progress. Buddha was also an advocate of Yoga and, as already stated, laid the greatest stress on it with its preliminaries, right conduct, etc. which might be regarded as making an individual fit for the exercise of mind and body that it involved, while he discouraged the mortifications which he regarded as useless. It was rendered simpler and more popular, while to this method of spiritual culture he made a contribution of his own in which the realization of impermanence of the world, the absence of soul as an indestructible and permanent entity, and the existence of suffering in all worldly affairs, led to a habitual practice of the *astāngika* mārga and the attainment of bliss by the dispersal of ignorance *(avidyā)* the root cause of misery.

From the facts stated above it will be manifest that the way of life that the Buddha looked upon as the path to Nirvāṇa was a good deal similar to the life of the *vānaprasthas* and Yatis. The wanderings of the yatis combined with the comparatively stationary life of the *vānaprasthas* within an absolute non-attachment to the worldly matter were engrated into a monkish organization with right conduct and simplified Yoga as their methods of sādhana, the radical difference lying in the fact that while the vānprasthaṣ and the yatis recognised the authority of the Vedas and the former performed simplified forms of sacrifices and rituals. The Buddhist monks cut off absolutely their connection with the Vedas, the authority of which they discarded outright.

We are now in a position to enumerate the external causes and circumstances that helped the wide spread propagation of Buddhism during the period from the first preachings of Buddhism by its founder to the reign of the emperor Aśoka when the religion spread over a very large portion of the sub-continent of India and even over parts of countries laying outside India.

The commanding personality of the Buddha, his self sacrifice, the strength of his character, his spiritual attainments, his supersensual vision, and the occasional manifestations of miraculous powers[42] served in a great degree to convince the people of his spiritual greatness and made them attach importance to his words. A.B. Keith attributes the vast success of Buddhism not so much to the merits of the religion as to the personality of the founder . He says that the founder of Buddhism must rank as one of the most commanding personalities ever produced by the eastern world."[43]

The character and personality of the Buddha's immediate disciples such a Sāriputta, Mogglāna, Mahākassāpa, Mahākaccāyana, Punna Mantaniputta Ānanda were also a powerful factor in the propagation of Buddhism. Their excellencies are mentioned sometimes by Buddha himself and sometimes by their brother monks. Sāriputta is described as excelling all in wisdom, self-control, and virtue, well composed in his inner self, dwelling on the highest planes of thought, expert in the knowledge of the doctrines and possession capacity for preaching persuasively[44]. Moggeāna was valiant, self controlled and possessed of super normal powers and able to raise the disciples to the highest stages of moral and spiritual progress,[45] Mahākassapa was the foremost in the ascetic ways which Buddha permitted as a concession to the tendencies of the age, self-sacrificing, and loving to dwell remote from men; Māhakaccāyana was a great expositor of dhama;[46] Punna Mantaniputta was an appealing preacher; and ānanda was the foremost bhikkhu in erudition, morally watchful, steadfast, versed in the sacred lore, and eloquent. The qualities mentioned are no doubt but hints that they were present in more than ordinary degree in the character of the monks, though it should not be supposed that the requisite qualities required for a monk but not mentioned above were absent in them. The monks were all at one in their zeal for the propagation of the religion, in the strength of which they had answering belief, and to the founder of which they all bore the highest reverence. This was the bond that combined them and their followers into a closely compact body to march on in the path of duty prescribed by the Buddha and to materialize His wishes by progagating His doctrines. The earnestness with which the first generation of the Buddha's disciples performed their duties can be best described by comparing it to the zeal which the Christian apostles did their share of work by practising and spreading doctrines promulgated by Christ.

The Buddhist leaders in the generation following the immediate disciples of Buddha up to the region of Aśoka included likewise prominent characters who might well take their place by the side of his immediate disciples. The names of monks who took a prominent part in the deliberations of the church organization and maintained discipline, moral or otherwise, are many, but the biographical details of only a few of them are found in Buddhist literature. Among these few may be mentioned Siggava whose preseverance in the cause of the conversion of non-Buddhists to Buddhism is found on the description where he is said to have daily visited, with ultimate success, the house of a Brāhmaṇa for so long as eleven years to persuade his son with teachings and arguments to embrace the religion;[48] Sāmbhūta Sānavāsika whose zeal in the work of conversion carried him so far as Kashmir and Kandahar to preach and secure converts in those places.[49] Revata vastly learned and free from āsavas (moral impurities). Yasa extremely energetic in the work of consolidating the Buddhist doctrines for which the second council was convened, and also in eliminating the evils that the Vajjians were trying to introduce into the church organisation by modifying its rules;[50] Udena who was able to convert Ghtoamukha Brāhmaṅa after the death of Buddha and have an upaṭṭhānasālā built at pāṭaliputra by him;[51] Ūpagupta of the time of Aśoka who was highly intelligent and eloquent, was a pillar of strength to the Buddhist church. It was the charm of his character and personality that made Aśoka accept him as his spiritual preceptor and help the Buddhist organization by building monasteries and stūpas in numberless places and give donations for the maintenance of the monks and the spread of Buddhism. Materials are yet lacking for drawing up a list of energetic and religious workers like those already mentioned showing the period in which they worked, the prominent qualities by which they were distinguished, and the share of burden borne by them in regard to preaching and conversion. Such a list is sure to be very useful in giving a picture of the person upon whom rested the arduous task of extending the *temits* of conversion, and in drawing a sketch of the gradual spread of Buddhism.

It is supposed that Buddhism while in its full bloom lacked an organization possessing a central power that could co-ordinate and bring into a line the local units scattered throughout the length and breadth of the region over which Buddhism had spread. This supposition is not supported by full reasons and evidences because the very fact of the rapid and extensive spread ofBuddhism as well as the maintenance of its hold upon the country for such a long time gives the lie direct to such an inference. Though there was no central authority of the kind that we generally find in the organization with which we meet ordinarily, the central authority in the Buddhist organisation was derived from the invisible body of rules, prescribed by the Buddha and very minute in their instructions. This set of rules regulated the smallest details of monastic life and commanded the common respect and obedience from all the monks whatever might be the position occupied by them in the organizaion or in whichever locality they might be stationed.[52] The one or two instances of difference of opinion or quarrel or disobedience that are found in the Buddhist work are generally interpreted as signs of the weakness of the organization lacking a central authority, but when we remember that the central authority as pointed out above was of a different kind and was obeyed with great respect by all the monks on account of their living faith in the words of Buddha, we are led to look upon that interpretation as wrong. Observers of the development of the Buddhist religion might fall easily into the error of thinking that the defect which afterwards grew into a source of weakness lay in the constitution which was left without a governing body.[53] But it should be remembered that the founder of the Buddhist religion ought to be credited with the knowledge claimed as a matter of course by the present day writers of the story of the development of Buddhism. The fallacy that is often committed by writers in tracing the causes of the decline of a social or religious institution or organism lies in the fact that they find fault with a particular limb of the organization or a particular practice which was really a source of strength when the institution or the organisation was in its healthy state. If in old age a finger of a man is attacked by gangrene, are we justified in laying the blame and in finding fault with the existence of the very finger itself and tracing the cause of the decline to the possession of that limb by the man when he was young and healthy. Similarly, to say that the cause of the decline of Buddhism is to be found in the want of check upon the local sanghas while the whole Buddhist organisation with the mutual co-operation of the local sanghas was able to keep Buddhism in a flourishing state for so many centuries is to take as a cause of decline a thing which was a cause of its prosperity or at its worst but a neutral something upon which the real cause operated its ruin. In the question before us, the invisible but yet forceful authority to which it has been referred was existent though it was intangible, and it was the gradual deterioration of the twin faiths of the monks and the introduction of elements that chilled the warmth of their faiths that are really responsible for bringing about weakness in the very organization which in the heydey of the prosperity of Buddhism worked so well, strengthened by the devoted attachment of the believing monks to the invisible central authority of Buddha's words constituting the life of whole organization. What I want to going out so that the strength of the Buddhist religion with its organizations lay in the living faith and devotion of its followers and not so much in the structure through which the faith, the devotion were ordained by Buddha to be given a material shape. Buddha gave his best consideration to the details of the structure of the organization and even changed them or added to their number as soon as the suggestion made by his followers met with his approval. No mundane organization can be perfect and it is enough if the common necessities pertaining to the object for which it is founded are provided for. Buddha went much further than this and prescribed a vinaya which was meant to meet even the probably or minute exigencies of monastic life. Magada formed a part of the eastern mid land and it offered circumstances which were favourable for the growth of heterodox ideas. This would explain why Buddha's preachings could be caught more rapidly by the people than it could have been done in the Kuru Panchāla territory.[54] Moreover there are evidences in the pitakas that the organization of the Brāhmanical orders in Magadha and Videha was not so strong and well-knit as to resist effectively the progress of Buddhism. The members belonging to the community were not also so strong in dialectics as to defeat in argument Buddha or the more eminent of the Buddhist monks and several cases are recorded of debates between the Brāhmaṅas and the Buddhists in which the former could not defeat the latter by showing the hollowness of the logic underlying the arguments. The Brāhmaṇas of this part of the country are found in the Buddhist work to be tracing their descent from Brāhmaṇas of the northern portions of India (*Udicca*) which show the source of Brāhmanic purity, was looked upon as existing there and not in the region where Buddhism flourished at first.[55] The well-known reference of the Satapatha Brāhmana states the river Sadānirā as the limit beyond which lay areas of land which were made fit for habitation for Brāhmaṅas only insofar as the sacrificial fire was lit up by them for the performance of sacrifices. This sacrificial fire had stopped on the Sadānirā in its migration towards the east which pointed to that river as the boundary of the area that had some time before been considered as the sacred land. It therefore, stands out that the tract of country east of the river was inferior to lands in the west from the view point of Brāhmanic orthodoxy. One more noticeable feature is the predominance of the kṣatriyas. In the eastern lands by virtue of wealth and acquisition of learning which made them powerful enough to carry on reactionary moments as against the existing conditions of things as settled or desired by the Brāhmaṇas. It is very difficult to say how far the ksatriya origin of Śākya siṃha brought strength to this religious propaganda by virtue of this mere affinity of origin between him and the kṣatriyas of the place. To assert that this element was altogether absent in the forces which made them cluster under his religious flag would be perhaps going too far. But it should always be borne in mind that the innate strength and attraction of the Buddha's personality and the doctrines preached by him were so great as to put into shade the force of this element, specially when entrance into the Buddhist order meant a cleavage between the family origin and the new life that was brought into being.

The rapid *spread of Buddhism within a few centuries after its foundation is due to the fact the conversion of non Buddhists to Buddhist* was regarded as a part of the duty of the monks at the highest stage of their *spiritual developments.* The attainment of Nirvāṇa by a Buddhist may be the goal of monk, but to attain it without at the same time giving others the opportunity of realizing its importance and taking to the right course for reaching it has about it a taint of selfishness however slight. The means by which the highest can be known and tasted ought not to be the secret of the select few or of an individual. It should be given a wide publicity in order that all men from the highest to the meanest may have the opportunity of exercising his judgement and take to the way that leads to the highest goal of manhood. The miseries of this world are countless, and they weigh down the hearts of men constantly with their heavy weights. If the truths found by Buddha, the mean discovered by him can lessen them even temporarily it is certainly a blessing;

and the truths in fact profess to bring within reach of mortals permanent blessings. Those who have realized this truth in their lives cannot sit idle and look upon their fellow human beings with unconcern while the remedy is within their reach. It was this feeling of love and compassion that animated Buddha and the Buddhists to preach broadcast the truth of their religion in order that the groping humanity may know that there are saving truths which can be attained by particular ways of regulating life and thought. It was from this point of view of looking at proselytizing that the Buddhists drew their stimulus for activities in this direction, and we find the Hinayānist and, in a greater measure, the Mahayanists exercising their best energies for the propagation of their faith for the diffusion of general well-being and the alleviation of miseries incidental to human existence. The sacred books of the Buddhist from the Nikāyas downwards contain passages extolling the merits of preaching and conversion. The verse of the :ammapada (354) "dhammdanam., Sabbadānam .Jnati" testifies to the high esteem in which the duty of conversion was held by the Hināyanists. The scriptures of the Mahāyānists look at the propagation of the faith in the same light. In the Saundarānanda Kāvya, Nanda's duty is not finished by the attainment of his own Nirvāṇa. He wanders about with the object of bringing salvation to the distressed beings. The same work describes the Buddha as making the remark that all beings are under delusion, and it is Nanda'a supreme duty to preach to them the dhamma, for he will be a lesson to those who are steeped in worldly passions.[56] The śiksāsdmuccaya qutotes passages from the prajnāpāramitā, *saddharmapuṇḍarika*, candrapradipasūtra, and sāgaramati sūtra on the merit of preaching and doing it with discrimination.[57]

Conversion by the evagelical method marks out Buddhism as making a radical departure from the traditionary lines on which the Indian religions brought new adherents into their fold. The ways in which Hinduism extended the boundaries of its domain are peculiar to itself. Its methods of enlisting new recruits are in consonance with the caste system, its spirit of exclusiveness specially in religious matters and its power of slowly adapting itself to the changes effected by forces from within or without the process followed by it consisted in absorbing the new recruits into the Hindu society by attracting them slowly and imperceptibly to adopt more or less the social customs and practices of the Hindus and thus occupy a place within an existing caste or sub-caste, or form a new sub caste, as the case may be. The alteration of the religious views is left to follow the social absorption that gradually sets in. The early Jainas, discarding as they did the caste-system, were in a position to follow a course different from the traditional method of the Hindu, but the Buddhists struck out a radically different path. The conversion of a new adherent was done deliberately, and his embrace of the new faith was effected in a way that could be well marked as a change that was being made with a deliberate object. With the Buddhist these features were more prominent, but among the Hindus, the change was slow and imperceptible. It was no doubt the zeal of the founders of religions and their best disciples to share with other the blessings of the state they attained and the truths they realized that impelled them to take to missionary activities,. The radical departure made by the Buddhists from the traditional method was responsible for the rapid way in which Buddhism spread not only in India but also in the countries outside. The very first resolution made by Buddha after the attainment of the summun bonum was to become a religious preacher and save mankind from worldly cares and miseries, he went to Sārnāth to convert the five Brāhmaṅas, after whom he made many more converts. He formed them into a band of missionaries, of whom he was the leader. All writers upon Buddhism are faced with the difficulty to explain in what respect the teaching of Buddha differs from the highest phases of Brāhmaṅa thought. It is true that the distinction appeared clear enough to Buddha and his successors; but this was largely because the Brāhmaṅism against which they maintained their polemic was after all merely the popular aspect of Buddhism[58]. From the study of the Buddha's dialogues it may appear that he never encountered a capable exponent of the highest vedantic idealism, such a one as Yājnavalkya or Janaka. Gautama took exception to the Atmanistic terminology rather than its ultimate significance.[59] It appeared to Buddha and his followers then that the highest truths especially the truth embodied by Buddhists in the phrase An-ata, no soul-lay rather without than within the Brāhmanical circle.

Many times in the history of religions has the Protestants, having thus easily carried the outer defences of an orthodox faith, believed thus there remained no other citadel. It may be on the otherhand, that Gautam knew of the existence of such a Brāhman citadel where the truth was held, that the Atmān is 'not so, not so' but regarded the surrounding city as so hopelessly habituated to errors of thought and action, as to determine him rather to build upon a new site than to join hands with the beleaguered garrison.

We are told for example that Buddhism differs from Brāhmanism in its refutation of the "then current pessimistic idea that salvation could not be reached on earth and must be sought for rebirth in heaven".[60]

Apart from these metaphysical discussions, one must have to go into the details of socio-economic condition of the period under review. The political scenario plays rather an important role in the origin and spread of any philosophy. In the rise of Buddhism against Brāhmanism, the most inevitable factor which may appear to any historian, is the contradictions within Brāhmanism itself. The Brāhmanic religion during those periods was more rigid, more orthodox and more obstinate to any reform. On the otherhand, the socio-economic and political environment was getting changed with the passage of time. But Brāhmaṇas were not in a position to bring any change in the social hierarchy. This contradiction proved to be an important factor in the rise of Buddhism. Besides, personality of Buddha plays not any insignificant role in the origin of Buddhist philosophy.

The origin and quick spread of Buddhism may be taken as a reaction to the Brāhmanic cult. Buddhism directly concerns with the problems of human life and its logical and scientific solution. The philosophy of Buddhism was well demonstrated by Buddha in his own life. His own experiments were the conclusion of his doctrine. Buddha's search for truth, his means of attainment, and his method of preaching were based on his rational approach and practical experience.

The advent of the Buddha with a new vigour in the spiritual and cultural thought of India was a historical necessity. Social, political and religious movement of India, before his advent, urgently demanded reformation and revolution of the traditional Indian culture based mainly on spiritual experiences. The Buddha had his own experiences, an experience which was noble, at the same time traditional in character.[61] To understand this unique position of Buddhism which represents the Indian culture in its entirety we should have an idea of the background of its origin.

Politically North eastern India was divided into sixteen Mahājanpad in the Buddist & Jaina literature. Some of the political heads of these Jana-pads were in constant conflict with one another, in most cases maintaining their own sovereignty over their respective states.[62] None of these states was powerful enough to over ride its neighbours of these 16 political units. Eight were ruled by hereditary kings and six by a democratic republican form of government. The Buddha was born in a family of republican chief whose status was no less than that of a king. While describing his own autobiography, Buddha said, "king Suddhodana my father... Kapilbastu his capital".[63]

Brāhmaṇical structure of the society with its division of four 'Varnas' and four 'Āśramas' was honoured as a principle, but there arose feeble noises of protest against the tradition in some places. The Buddha finally realised the situation and brought a radical change in certain matters which threatened the supremacy of the Brāhmanical rule over the society. The society was divided into four hereditary castes. The system was rigid having no chance of promotion from lower to higher caste on the basis of merit, neither was there any provision for degrading a higher caste to a lower one on the ground of demerit. The Brāhmins by birth had the privilege to taking prominent part in the society in religious matters, study of sacred texts and performances of sacrifices.

Far from it the Vedic cult of sacrifice was generally accepted as the religious practice by the majority of the Aryan Indians before the time of the Buddha. Most of the sacrifices aimed at the material gain for this birth or for merits leading to different heavens, the abodes of happiness after death. But neither the material happiness of this birth nor the heaven after death is permanent. In the very vedic literature, specially in some upaniṣads, the effects of their sacrifices were not highly valued. The seers of the upaniṣads laid stress on the permanent solution of the problem of life by renunciation and withdrawing the mind from the desire for happiness either in this world or in heaven. This is why the ascetic life was highly praised. Performance of the sacrifice was a monopoly of the Brahmins.

The Buddha'a doctrine was founded on the ground of *karma*, the responsibility being laid on the individual. It was a rational approach for transformation of life from a state of misery to the state of perfection. In the wilderness of doctrines and theories Buddha demonstrated a life which had been universally accepted by all people seeking solution to the fundamental problem of life. According to S. Radhakrishan:[64] "The Buddha utilised the Hindu inheritance to connect some of its expressions, he came to fulfil and not to destroy. Buddhism appeared in India with the true spirit of Hinduism which aimed at the perfection of life through renunciation, contemplation and meditation as demonstrated in the life of the Buddha".[65]

Here Radhakrishnan attempts to equate Buddhism with Hinduism. But Radhakrishan's conception of Buddhism as a naturally of Hinduism shows his prejudices about the Hindu religion. If Buddhism was not a departure from vedic religion why Buddha had to meet the resentment of the Brāhmaṇas? Needless to say, that Buddhism came out of reaction of the vedic sacrifices and its varṇa rigidity.

The materialist conception regarding the early spread of Buddhism is associated with the use of iron. The plenty use of iron in eastern U.P. And Northern Bihar facilitated the spread of Buddhism. The use of iron made it possible to make weapons on the one hand and involve large scale production on the other. With the use of iron implements deforestations started and the lands were now being used for production. Vaiśyas were involved in producing activities. When production increased, gradually they grew richer. In this position, naturally they could have sought a position in the society as after the industrial revolution the rising middle class fought for social status; on the other hand, use of iron helped the warrior class who were in a continuous struggle against the Brāhmanas. It is not without reason that in the 6th century Magadhan kings were more powerful. Now the concept of state came into being and thus Buddhism become state religion at the time of Aśoka.

REFERENCE

1. B.M. Barua, *Pre-Buddhistic Indian Philosophy*, pp. 193-94.
2. T.W.R. Davids, *Buddhist India* ; pp. 83-84.
3. Cf. "For the first time in the history of the world, it proclaimed a salvation which each man could gain for himself in this world, during this life, without the least refrence to God or to

gods, either great or amall." Rhy Davids, *Habbert Lectures;* p. 29.

4. *Majjh Nik.* II. p. 169, *Digh Nik*; I, *Tevijja Sutta*; Oldenberg's Buddha; pp. 172-73.
5. Digh Nik. I. p. 138.
6. R. Fick; *Die Sociale Gliederung*; etc. transl. By Dr. S.K. Maitra.
7. Prof. E.W. Hopkins, *Religions of India*; p. 188.
8. Digh. Nik; II pp. 316. ff.
9. Ibid I. pp. 127 ff.
10. Barua, *pre-Buddhistic Indian Philosophy*; p. 193.
11. *Digh Nik.,* Brahmajāla *sutta*; transl. by Rhys Davids.
12. *Rv.* I. 164. 27. VII. 68. 9, IX. 80.2, X.60 II, 87,16.
13. *Av;* III 30.1, XVIII. 3.4, 4.9.
14. *Dictionary of Pali Proper Names* 1; 337.
15. *SN.* I. 75-76.
16. *Ibid.* 76.
17. *Ibid*; 76.
18. *Ibid*; 76.
19. Davids, the Dialogues of Buddha; part I, pp. 17.25; cf. Sutta Nıpata (S.B.E.); pp. 48-50, Majjh Nik; p. 82 where Buddha expatiated on the inefficacy of sacrifice (Yajña).
20. An article presented by a Japanese scholar in the 44th session of the Indian History Congress, Burdwan, 1983.
21. Digh Nik,. III pp. 49, 50, 223, 234; Majjh Nik, I, pp,. 283, 284, 359 ff.
22. R.S. Sharma, *Ancient India*, p. 56.
23. *Rg. Veda*, Puruṣa-sukta.
24. "The thought that a brāhmanas does not occupy a special place by reason of his birth but that virtue alone constitutes, a true Brāhmaṇā occurs also in the Jatakas. "Dr. R. Fick, *social Gliederung*, etc. transl. p. 20.
25. *Dīgh. Nik;* iii. pp. 80.

26. *Digh. Nik; I. Amtattha sutta; Majjh Nik*; ii, *Assatāyana sutta*, pp. 147. *Madhura* sutta, pp. 83. Ang. Nik; i. p. 162.
27. *Vinaya pitaka*; vol. II p. 239.
28. Jatakas; III, 194 ff.
29. Digh Nik, I, *Tevijja suttanta*; p. 239; Barua's *pre-Buddhistic Indian Philosophy*. p. 193, 243, "All the thinkers in the neo-Vedic period agreed in estimating the four Vedas and Vedic sciences as the lower knowledge.
30. T.W.R. Davids, *Buddhist India*, p. 192. Anand Coomarswamy, *Buddha and the Gospel of Buddhism*, p. 198.
31. Rhys Davids, *Dialogues of the Buddha*; I. p. 24.
32. Max Mūllar, Anceint Sanskrit, Literature, pp.43-44.
33. Digh Nik.; *Brahmajala suttanta and Kevaddhe suttant*a.
34. Majjh Nik; I. pp. 77. 242-246.
35. Rhys Davids, Dialogues of the Buddha; I. p. 219.
36. A. Coomarswamy, *op. cit:* p. 199 Buddhism differs from Brāhmanism in its refutation of the "then currrent persimistic idea that salvation could not be reached on earth, and must therefore be sought for in rebirth in heaven." T.W., Rhys Davids, *Early Buddhism*. p. 55.
37. *Majjh* Nik; i., p. 242-244.
38. Buddha'a atttitude towards the Brahmanic ascetic practices is set forth in many places in the *Nikāyas,* one of which is, for instance, —"An ascetic who has adopted the mode of taking food in the manner of a dog or cow (kukkuravatika or govatika), takes rebirth on account of his penance in this life either as a dog or a cow and if he longs to be reborn in the world of gods as a result of his penances in this life, he is doomed to perdition for the wrong view he holds." *Majjh. Nik.*; I.p. 239. II, pp. 387, 388.
39. E.G. *Dīgh.* Nik.; III, pp. 42 ff.
40. Warren's Budhism in Translations, pp. 282, 283.
41. *Sutta Nipata* (S.B.E.) ; pp 167-74. "The different school of philosophy contradict each other, they proclaim different truths, but the truth is only one. As long as the disputations are going on, so long will there be strife in the world."

42. *Vinaya*; I. pp. 16, 25 ff.
43. A.B. Keith, *Buddhist philosophy, p.* 147.
44. Rhys Davids, *Psalms of the Brethren*; pp. 69, 388, 402 & 390 fn.
45. *Ibid.* p. 390 fn.
46. *Ibid.* pp. 386-387
47. Rhys Davids, op cit., 352-353.
48. *Mahāvaṁśa*; ch. V.
49. Edkins; *Chinese Buddhism;* p. 67.
50. *Mahāvaniśa*; ch. IV.
51. *Majjh.* Nik; II, p. 163.
52. *Digh, nik*; II, p. 154 yo vo „Ānanda mayā dhammoca Vinaya ca desito paññatto so vo mama accayena sattha; Majjh. Nik , III, p. 10. Ananda explains to Gopaka Moggalana about the headship of the church; "Na kho mayam, Brāhmana, appatisarana, sappatisarana mayam Brahmana, dhammapatisarana ti Vadesi."
53. Romila Thapar, *Decline and fall of the Maurya Empire*; p. 89.
54. Hastings. *Encyclopaedia of Religion and Ethics*; III, p. 540.
55. R. Fick, Sociale Gliederung etc. Transl;. pp. 34, 40-213.
56. *Saundarada Kāvya*; Sarga 18 Sloks, 54-58.
57. *Siksasamuccaya (Bendall's* translation); pp 310-11.
58. Coomarswamy, *Buddha and the Gospel of Buddhism;* p. 197.
59. Ibid.
60. T.W. Ryhs Davis, *Early Buddhism.* p. 55.
61. S. Dhar, *Netaji Institute for Asian studies, Monograph* series 1, p. 1.
62. This conception of Buddhist emergence has been duquted by D.D. Kosambi, R.S. Sharma, Romila Thapar.
63. Digha-Nikaya, Mahapadana Suttanta 14.3.30 Also see, S. Dhar, p. 2.
64. *Mundaka Upanisad,* 1. 2. 7.
65. S. Dhar, *op. cit.* p. 11.;

Chapter III

Beginnings of Buddhist Art in the Pre-Aśokan Period (532 B.C.—269 B.C.)

"The history of Buddhist Art", according to Vogel[1] "does not really commence until the reign of the great Aśoka, Circa 269 B.C two centuries and a quarter after the Buddha's nirvāṇa". As the pre-eminent Buddhist emperor of India Aśoka zealously made efforts to propagate the Buddhist creed for which purpose he built various stambhas or lats which may be regarded as the earliest historical specimens of Indian art. Under the royal support of Aśoka Buddhist art received a forceful fillip and the glorious tradition initiated by him continued upto the times of Ajanta. But it does not mean that Buddhist or Indian art and architecture originated in the times of Aśoka, for considering the highly developed style and polish applied to Mauryan pillars it is possible to ascribe a long tradition to Indian architecture and culture.[2] What the Mauryan era signified is the substitution of stone for wood which was the common material used for building purposes. Wood being highly susceptible to the vagaries of the Indian climate, no specimen of the Pre-Mauryan art worth their name have come down to us and the history of art in pre-Mauryan India remains, in the words of Foucher, "philologically a blank page, archaeologically an empty show-case."[3]

Buddhist art received its incentive from a king like Aśoka but essentially it owes its origin to the enthusiasm and efforts of the Buddhist laity. Buddhist art is fundamentally the art of the people. It reflects the ideas and ideals, ambitions, joys and fears of the Buddhist laymen. Though essentially religious in character, it is nevertheless comprehensive in its scope. Early Indian art is always "utilitarian" in conception for the ancient Indians never believed in art for arts sake and works of art in India have always been produced in response to a specific demand and that demand was a transfiguration in stone of a sublime religious urge.[4] Thus Buddhist art, being an art produced for a people newly conscious of their distinct identity shows us the vibrant life which the people lived in all its vividness.

The beginning of Buddhist art may then be sought in the times when the laity were united with saṁgha of the four-quarters with a singleness of purpose and harmonious understanding. According to Foucher, Buddhist art found its origin in the custom of the devotees going on pilgrimages to the holy places of Buddhism. Human nature, he argues, is such that visitors when on visits to places of interest always persist in bringing back mementoes from such places of interest.[5] And when such places are invested with religious significance the need for mementoes is more urgently felt. Thus the Buddhist ley-devotees visiting Sārānātha or the Lumbini forest must naturally have wished to bring back from there such emblems as would constantly remind them of their visits and keep afresh the memory of the Master.

But apart from these commemorative tablets there must have been in existence buildings in Vihāras which were built with a different end in view. We are told of Anāthapiṇḍaka building the *Jetavana Vihāra* for the Buddha of which scene a carving is found on the railings of Bārhut.[6] Anathapiṇḍaka on going to Srāvasti thought of erecting a building where the Buddha could comfortably stay in peace and quietitude. He approached the prince Jeta in this connection and bargained for the purchase of his garden. The prince stipulated that Anāthapinḍaka could have the garden if he paid in exchange as many pieces of coins as would cover the entire plot.

This being done Anāthapinḍaka built "dwelling rooms, and retiring rooms, and storerooms (over the gateways) and service halls, and halls with fire-places in them, and store houses (outside the Vihāra) and closets and cloisters and halls for exercise and wells, and sheds for the wells and bath-rooms, and halls attached to the bath-rooms and ponds, and open roofed sheds. The *cullavagga* of the Vinaya Piṭaka narrates to us the incidents which appear to be connected with the earliest of such works. A merchant of Rājagṝha[7] seeing that the Bhikkhus, being without buildings, were forced to stay wherever they could expressed a desire to build dwellings for them. The Bhikkhus declined the offer because the Buddha had not given them permission to accept any such dwellings.

The matter was reported to the Buddha who then accorded the necessary permission in the following words; "I allow you, oh Bhikkhus, abodes of five kinds Vihāras, *addhayogas*, storeyed *dwellings, attics, caves*." Thereafter the merchant of Rājagṝha put up sixty dwelling-places in one day. This he did "for the sake of heaven." These sixty dwelling places were dedicated to the "saṁgha of the four quarters."[8]

Buddhist art evolved in answer to a specific demand which was to satisfy the religious urge of the people. On the other hand it fulfilled a real need. It proved a very valuable centre for propagating the Buddhist faith most effectively. It also served as a potentially cohesive force in uniting the Buddhist lay community with more integration and solidarity. We know from some Sāmchi and Bārhut inscriptions that village committees were formed to help building the railings of the stupas at Bārhut and Sāmchi.[9]

These Buddhist places of worship not only provided external symbols—a long felt need for the laity—but also brought them together in a group bound by common ideals and aspirations. The artist, on his part, being thoroughly imbued with Buddhist ideals could portray their innermost thoughts and feelings. Smith[10] opined an artist is the expression rather of collective then of individual thought?..." The Buddhist artist living in a society which piously turned its lofty thoughts towards the Buddha and his inspiring life and being himself endowed with a "projective" imagination of his own could reflect the ideals of the times in which he lived and thus liberated the synthesising forces of art for the unification and edification of his people.

Buddhist art had another advantage and it lay in the liberal tendencies adopted by the patrons in the selection of the workmen. Buddhism, being itself protest against the cast system, naturally ignored the differences of caste. In consequence the Buddhist art patrons had a wider scope for selection of artists.[11] The artists, on their part, coming from diverse strata of society and representing diverse environment brought with them a refreshing variety to bear upon their artistic productions. Further, as all of them were, in all probability, Buddhist or at least deeply imbued with Buddhistic ideals could easily and faithfully represent the religious feeling and ideals of their patrons. Again execution of such artistic edifices being considered works of merit the believing artists could work with burning zeal and an unparalleled singleness of purpose. All these factors combined to produce a gigantic pageant which we now call Buddhist art.

All Buddhist art, from the point of view of the laity, could be divided into two distinct groups. Under the first would fall all such buildings as were utilitarian in purpose, like cells, caves, Vihāras and parks and the other groups would comprise commemorative structures like *stupas* with their railings.

It is generally traditional to begin the history of art with the reign of Aśoka[12] for a really cogent history of art in India could only begun with the glorious rule of Aśoka. It has been seen earlier that Indian art had a tradition going much more into antiquity than the age of the Mauryas. There are, however very few remains of pre-Mauryan art that have survived. Because wood was the building material which is perishable which could be definitely termed as Pre-Mauryan and preserved in a condition which makes the assessment of their worth practical. The edifice known as Jarāsandha-ki-baithakā at Rājagir is distinctly pre-Aśokan.[13]

Besides this, several other specimens could also be attributed to a pre-Mauryan times. These may be described as the parakhām statue of *Yakṣa,* two Patna *Yakṣa* statues, the Besnagar *Yakṣi* statue, the Chhargaon Nago statue, the Mathurā seated Yakṣa, the Patna female chauri-bearer, the upper part of the Baroda colossal *Yakṣa* and the Besnagar *kalpavrkas.*[14] Compared to the Aśokan specimens these figures are crude and lacking in finish but they show the trends in which artistic tendencies were progressing.

But with Aśoka Buddhist art comes into its own. If the credit of invigorating Buddhist ārt is to be given to Aśoka then Buddhism must be attributed the inspiration which formed the motive force of all Aśokan artistic representations. "Aśoka..." observes Havell,[15] raised the technique of arts employed by brāhmanical ritualism on to a higher intellectual plane and made the fine arts a potent instrument in national education and in his propagation of the Buddhist faith..." The teaching of the Buddha, according to the same authority[16] served a great impulse to the development of Indian art, "widening the intellectual outlook, and co-relating the abstract ideas and spiritual vision of the vedic age with human conduct and the realities of life."

Asokān monuments, for the purpose of description and evaluation, could be divided into three groups: (a) stūpas (b) caves and (c) pillars.

According to Buddhist tradition Aśoka was responsible for building 84,000 stupas.[17] The statement though exaggerated out of all proportion contains a germ of truth. We are told that the relics of the Buddha's body were distributed first after his death and the second distribution took place in Aśoka's reign.[18] Over some relics he must have built stupas at various places. The Samchi stupa in the earliest stage belonged to the Aśokan age.[19] Likewise to Aśoka must be attributed the stupa at Sārnath.[20] These stupas were probably built of bricks over which successive generations added some portions resulting in the grand edifices discernible today in their ruins. These stupas must have contained some relics of the Buddha's body or of his prominent disciples.[21] Aśoka himself speaks of his having enlarged the stupa of Konagamana, a former Buddha.[22]

The earliest historical cave of India can be attributed to the 12th regnal year of Aśoka.[23] The Karna Chopar cave was excavated in the 19th year of his reign. These caves are carved out of a solid piece of rock, generally of granite.[24] The frontage contains a door with sloping jambs which are evidently a copy of the wooden prototypes.[25] The Lomasa Rishi cave has over its door a carving showing a flowery fringe with another showing a fringe of elephants.[26]

The Barabar group of caves situated in an isolated range of granite hills on the left bank of the Phalgu river in the Gaya district are a prominent example of early cave architecture. "They are seven in number, and though deffering in plan, are all similar in character and evidently belong to the same age. Their dimensions are considerable."[27] Both internally and externally they are plain and devoid of all artistic decoration and though they are the "smallest and least ornamented of any to be found in India, it still must have required a strong religious impulse to induce men to excavate even caves 30 to 40 feet in length in the hard granite rock, and to polish their interiors to the extent that some of them are finished and all probably were intended to have been."[28]

The pillars of Aśoka which "merit our attention and admiration as monuments of engineering ability, perfect examples of the highest skill of the stone cutter and vehicles of a brilliant display of fine art" form a distinct landmark in the evolution of Indian architecture and sculpture.[29] The list of Aśokan pillars consists of about 10 monoliths as follows : (a) Delhi-Topra, (b) Delhi-Mirath (c) Allahabad (d) Lauriya-Areraja (e) Lauriya Nandangarh (f) Rampurva, (g) Sānchi (h) Sārnāth (i) Rummindei and (j) Nigliva.[30] These monoliths are of highly polished sandstone over 30 feet in height. The columns have a tapering appearance and the top is surmounted with a capital variously described as bell-capital or an inverted lotus. The capital supports the figure of an animal, either a lion or a bull. The capital projects on all sides of the shaft and "the underside of the projecting portion is relieved with an ornament" and some design while "the bell itself is decorated with conventional lotus petals."[31] The animals display a vibrant spirit and possess a majesty all their own revealing the familiarity of the artist with object of nature. The massive appearance of the shaft and weight pose to us problems of considerable engineering interest and compel even the most sceptical critic to speak with full warmth in admiration and praise about the artistic merit of these monoliths.

To make a comprehensive account of the development of a Buddhist art in Bihar, it is needed to rely more and more on the ruins and sites which have been located throughout the different stages of history. Needless to say that much endeavour in this respect has been made by the British administrators and historians time and again. Bihar enjoys a formidable place in history especially at the time when Buddhism made its mark on this soil. Lord Buddha was closely associated with Magadh because Magadhan kings even patronised and promoted the ideology of Buddha. That is why several architectural developments did take place in Magadh and its adjoining areas.

The relics of Buddhism still existing in Bihar may be divided into five groups: (1) ruins of temples (2) those of monasteries or Vihāras (3) votive stupas (4) figures and sculptures (5) inscriptions.

The Temples seem to have varied in size and splendour at different epochs in the history of the religion to which they belong.[32] Amongst the earlier temples are those of Rājgir, Dāpthū, and the Indra-Saila peak and amongst the more modern, those of Bargaon. The most ancient of the temples are remarkable for the extreme simplicity of their construction. They usually consisted of an outer court, varying in size from fifteen to twenty-five feet, the wall of which were composed of enormous bricks of rare solidity. The roof of the building was generally nine or ten feet high, sometimes more, somctimes less, and consisted of slabs of granite or other stone, placed close to each other, and supported by pillars of the same material. The capitals of the pillars were generally separate from the shaft, and of such size and form as to render the weight of the roof less difficult to sustain. Their shape was generally either cruciform or oblong. This court generally led to an inner chamber or shrine, smaller and less lofty than the vestibule, but of similar shape and construction. In the centre of this is generally to be found the figure of Buddha. Carvings were often arranged round the walls of the outer apartment but apparently merely for the purpose of ornament. The roof was generally covered with brick and probably surmounted by a low cupola or turret of the same material. The lintels of the door way were generally composed of basalt slabs, rudely carved with a bold geometrical pattern having one or more figures of Buddha in the centre. The brick work appears uniformly to have been plain, but remarkably uniform, the outside edges being reduced to a level by the chisel. As an illustration of the older type of Buddhist temple it may be mentioned the large one discovered in the side of the Baibhar hill at Rājgir.[33] A great number of the pillars are literally embedded in the brick work of the wall. This feature is also observable in the excavated building at the normal-kind, and the series of temples at Dāpthū.[34] The more modern temples present a striking contrast to the more ancient ones. The walls of these buildings were adorned with the most exquisitely moulded brick work; the facade was lavishly ornamented with pillared vestibules, and the richest sculptures which art could produce; the roof was crowned with a majestic spire or cupola abounding in profuse decoration in brick, plaster and basalt; and the doors and windows were surrounded with bands of ace like carving. The excavated temple at Bargaon affords a striking example of religious architecture of the Buddhists from 450 A.D. to 900 A.D.

'Raised a few feet above the plain was an evenly paved court, as near as possible one hundred feet square. This court was surrounded by halls and buildings of every description on all sides except the eastern, and these doubtless served as the dwelling-places, refractory, of the recluses of the convent. In the centre of the court rose an enormous temple, eighty feet long at the base on each side and consisting of a series of several storeys tapering to a point each about fourteen feet above the other.[35] The main fabric was composed of enormous bricks, each about one foot three inches in length, three inches thick, and ten inches wide, placed so close together that the cement which joined them is barely visible.[36] The first two storeys of the building were uncovered, and are now almost as perfect as when Huen-tsang saw them fourteen hundred years ago.[37] In order to preserve every detail in describing this remarkable building, we will take it side by side. The great entrance was towards the east (a custom still observed in the construction of the Buddhist temples of Tibet), and was faced by a terrace of stone fifty feet in length and composed of two rows of sandstone slabs, the first decorated by a simple triangle in the centre, the second carved with a very beautiful geometrical pattern.[38] These stones vary in length from seven to three feet, and are as near as possible a foot square.[39] In the centre of this terrace, which is about six feet in front of the main building, is a dight of three steps exactly ten feet in length.

The construction of Buddhist temple may not be reduced to any certain period but the art of construction flourished in different periods and in different regions. In Bhagalpur, at Barantpura, there is a temple of goddess Chandi built on the ancient site of a Buddhist temple.[40]

Near Bela in Gaya district there are remains of temples, Hindus as well as Buddhist of which only broken images had survived. The construction of the temple suggests that it may be of the pre-Aśokan period. The temple was first seen by Beglar in 1872. Of them a 'linga' is credited with a superstition that in spite of all attempts it could not be moved from its place. Beglar here also saw a piece of Buddha image with the usual Buddhist creed formulae inscribed on it.[41]

According to the Buddhist tradition, immediately after enlightenment, Buddha walked to and fro, near the sacred tree, for seven days. The spot, where he walked so, become sacred quite early and a shrine was built over it perhaps, by the noble lady Kurangi in about 1st century B.C.[42] In Buddhist tradition the shrine is called as "*jewel walk-shrine*". The spot is situated close to the north of the Boddhi tree. The remains of the ancient shrine now consist, of a long brick platform, 53' x 3'6" and about 3' in height, bearing on its upper surface, carvings of two lotus flowers each representing, serially a foot-print of the Buddha.[43]

It is said that in the fourth week after enlightenment Buddha sat cross-legged on a spot meditating with a view to formulate the '*Abhidhamma-naya*' or high modes of exposition of his doctrines and this spot is specially held sacred by the Buddhist:

there are other sacred spots within the precincts of the great temple similarly associated with other incidents in the Buddha's life immediately before and after enlightenment. But it has not been possible to correctly identify these spots.[44]

At Dāpthu in the Patna district a site of temple has been noticed though there is a lot of controversy over it. Buchānan refers to a large mound with a ruined mud fort built by a Brāhmin widow. South-east of the fort was the largest temple at the place locally called as that of Pārsvānātha i.e. a jaina Tirthankara, though in fact it may have been a Buddhist shrine,[45] as surmised by Buchanan from the carvings and sculptures lying amongst the ruins.

A site of the Buddhist temple, though very small but quite significant has been noticed by Beglar in his report for 1872-73 and mentions its name as Bishanpur Ghenjan.[46] The village is situated on the Morhar river about five miles west of Makhdumpur railway station. A number of sculptures were discovered here some of which were removed to the Indian museum, Calcutta of which four broken images of the Buddha and two pedestal of similar images are preserved at the site underneath a modern shed erected by the archaeological department of Govt. Of India.[47] The construction of the temple suggests that it may be traced back to the 4th century B.C.

At Gurpa hill in the Gaya district, on a small boulder along one of the walls of the tunnel are some Buddhist images, one representing the Buddha, now without the head 8' in height and another in 'bhūmisparśa-mudrā.'[48] On the top of this peak were noticed two miniature shrines, a number of Buddhist statues and some small vative stupas. The images include figures of the Buddha and the Goddess Tārā, some of them bearing inscriptions containing the usual Buddhist creed formulae. The image of Tārā with Buddha is the product of the third or fourth century A.D. especially after the coming of the Kushānas.

Karangja is mentioned as the name of a division in the district by Buchnan, who noticed a temple of Dakshina Bhawānī. He refers, in all , to three brick temples, with doomed roofs built inside a walled enclosure of them one contained an image of Kālī, another a linga and the third an image of a deity locally called as Bhairava, but Buchanan thought it to be of the Buddha.[49]

In later Buddhist pantheon Tārā is very much associated with Buddhism. In Buchana's time, a village named Kiśpa near Gaya, the place had been known for its temple dedicated to Goddess Tārā. In 1872-73 Beglar noticed the temple of Tārā-Devī and discovered the enshrined image to be of a male deity with an inscription on its halo, and thought it to be a Buddhist image.[50] The temple consists, in plan of the sanctum only, but it is likely it had pillared hall or mandap infront of it.[51]

In 1872, Broadley discovered some antiquarian remains. At Mubarakpur in the Patna district he discovered Buddhist idols, more than fifty in number. Several to them were unfinished and others scarcely begun. Broadley mentions that idols may be traced back to the Mauryan period. The site impressed him much and he remarked that "Mubarkpur has been the site of a sculptor's studio."[52]

The architectural perfection of Buddhistic art may be seen in some of the temples and caves buildings at Nālandā near Rājgīr. Nālandā with which the Buddhist site has been so identified, if one of the most famous places in the history of Buddhism. The Pāli texts of the Buddhists contain numerous references to it under the various names of Nala, Nalaka, Nalakagram, and Nālandā. It is however curious that the place is not to be found mentioned in early Hindu literary works, such as the epics and the purānas.[53]

The excavations however reveal that the foundation of the great tradition of learning and monasticism, for which

Nālandā later came to be known all over the Buddhist world, were laid sometimes during the fourth and fifth centuries. From this time Nālandā rose to the fame and importance it acquired afterwards.

A site at Narawat amongst the Rājgīr hills is within the boundary of Gaya district and its antiquity and ruins are found noticed only by Buchanan in about 1812. Buchanan noticed near the village "several heaps of bricks of very little elevation" with many defaced images and several rude pillars.[54] A broken lower half of an image of Buddha was enshrined in the temple[55] as seen by Buchanan.

It is said in the Buddhist Mahāparinibbāna-Sutta that some time before his death, the Buddha had noticed a fort being constructed by the side of the village "Pātali" under orders of the ambitious king Ajātaśatru of Rājgrha.

Kittoe mentions the name of the place Pnawan (Gaya) where he noticed a "large Buddha temple in ruins, but sufficiently entire to enable a good plan to be made of it ..." He calls it as "handsome" and the most perfect of any I have met with.[56] It possessed the most striking picture of the style, viz. a solid round lower with a niche to each of the cardinal points, ornamented with figures of four or five Buddhas.

Besides these temples, we have some references of ancient Buddhist forts, roads, embankments and caves. Among the caves a few of them are notable. At Giriak, 13 miles south of Biharsharif, the ancient ruins were noticed and described by Buchanan in 1861-62.[57] Local tradition associates the place with the epic king Jarasandha of Rājgīr.[58] Nearly this place, the village Jethian is situated on the western side of the valley south-west from Rājgīr. The antiquity of this area first noticed in 1871 by Cunningham, who identified Jeṭhian with Yashtivana of the Buddhist tradition as quoted by Huen-tsang.[59] Though

Cunningham does not seem sure regarding the site to which period it belonged.

Several Buddhist sites have been identified of the period under study. Broadley had identified with Indra-Śila-guhā of the Buddhist tradition mentioned by Huen-tsang. Broadley had attributed it to a Buddhist monastery" and he found here Chaityas, portions of gate-ways. A famous Buddhist site at Bodh-Gaya is perhaps more remarkable because this place is very much associated with the life of the Buddha. Remains of a massive stone railing are at present found enclosing the great temple on the three sides along its plinth and basement.[60] The total height of the railing is about 10 feet and part of the railing is of sandstone while part is of granite. Under the Boddhi tree was placed, perhaps by the emperor Aśoka, a polished sandtone slab called as *vajrāsana* or "diamond throne" representing the seat of the Buddha and around it was, later in the 1st century B.C., erected a stone railing.[61]

To conclude the development of Buddhist art in India, here it is needed to write a little on the trends of art during the period. The artistic efforts of ancient India, especially of the early Buddhist period, are only slightly connected with the general history of art. From the very first two schools are met with, one of them, the older-borrows Persian forms, and, indirectly, some Greek ones, and confined as it is to India, subsequently becomes the basis of all that may be called Indian art-Buddhist as well as Brāhminical, the religious character, so deeply rooted in national life of the Indian races, has also continued to be the guiding principle in their art.

The art of ancient India has always been a purely religious one, its architecture as well as the sculpture, which has always been intimately connected there with, was never and nowhere employed for secular purposes. It owed its origin to the growth of a religion which has been called in Europe Buddhism from the honorary title of its founder—"the Buddha"—the enlightened one.[62]

The sculpture of ancient India, originating as it did in religious tendencies and destined to serve religious purposes, could only follow its own immediate purpose in sacred representations. By Gandhara sculptures are designated the numerous images, pillars excavated from the ancient ruins of Buddhist monasteries and stupas on the north-west frontier of India.[63] They have been variously styled as Graeco- Buddhist, Āryan & Indo-Greek. They are all but entirely connected with Buddhist iconography.[64] and many of them manifest some western or classical influence.

REFERENCE

1. Vogel, *Buddhist art;* p. 16.
2. As is well known there is absence of specimens of monuments representing the several phases of Pre-Mauryan art but there is enough evidence in literature to indicate that art in India had a long history even before the Mauryan period. We have literary references to royal palaces built on a thousand pillars, assembly halls, towns and cities etc. For details see V.S. Agrawala, Indian Art; pp. 103-08.
3. Foucher, *The Beginnings of Buddhist Art*; p. 10.
4. Coomarswamy, *Indtroduction to Indian Art;* p. V.
5. Foucher, *op. Cit;* p. 12.
6. Barua, *Barhut inscriptions;* p. 59, S B.E. XX p. 187.
7. *Cullavagga; vi, i.* P. 2; S.B.E. XX p. 157.
8. D.R. Patil, The Antiquarian *remains of Bihar*, pp. 233-35.
9. Barua & Sinha, *Barhut inscriptions,* p. 14.
10. Smith, *Greek Art & national life,* p. 263.
11. Havell, a handbook of Indian Art; p. 20.
12. Grunwedel, Buddhist Art in India; p. 2. Also Bachhofer, *Early Indian sculpture*; p. 1.
13. Fergusson, *History of India & Eastern Architecture;* i. P. 175.

14. A Prakash, *The Foundation of Indian Art & Archaeology*; pp. 80-81.
15. Hàvell, *Ideals* of *Indian* Art; pp. 15-16.
16. *Ibid;* p. 13.
17. Legge, Travels of Fa-hien; p. 69.
18. Cf. Jayaswal, J.*B. O. R.S.* Xvii, p. 400 where he attributes 298 B.C. as the date of distribution.
19. Fergusson, History of Indian & Eastern Architecture; I. p. 68, Marshall and Voucher monuments of Samchi, I. P. 21, Havell, op. *Cit; p. 27.*
20. Marshall, & Foucher, *The monuments of Samchi;* p. 21.
21. *Ibid.*
22. Hultzsch, Inscriptions of Aśoka; p. 165.
23. Fergusson & Burgess, Cave Temples cf India; p. 38.
24. Fergusson & Burgess, Cave Temples of India; p. 41
25. *Ibid*; p. 40.
26. *Ibid*; p. 39.
27. *Ibid*; p. 38.
28. *Ibid*; p. 42.
29. "The monolithic pillars of columns rf Asoka" *Z.D.M.G.*,1911, p. 221.
30. *Ibid; 225.*
31. A.S.I., *New imperial series; vol.* IV, p. 9.
32. In Bihar one can notice numerous ruins of Buddhist temple and forts. At Alwara in Manbhum district, a large Buddhist temple remains include pieces of door-jambs with the seated Buddha figure earned on it. At *Amaithi* in Gaya district in about 1900 Stein noticed at the village shrine three old images. D.R. Patil, *op. Cit;* p. 2.
33. D.R. Patil, op. Cit; 3.
34. Ibid; p. 3.
35. A.M. Broadley, *The Buddhistic Remains of Bihar;* p. 13

36. *Ibid;* p. 14.
37. *Ibid;* pp. 14-15.
38. A.M. Broadley. *Op. Cit;* p. 14.
39. *Ibid;* p. 15.
40. *Bengal district gazetters and Bihar district gazetters;* (Bhagalpur), pp. 42, 162, 165.
41. Grierson, Notes on the district of Gaya; p. 21.
42. Buchanan, H. *An account of the District of Bihar and Patna*; p. 150. Cunningham, A. *Mahabodhi*; pp. 8-9.
43. Cunningham, A. *Op. Cit;* p. 9.
44. Cunningham, *op cit;* p. 34 ff D.R. Patil, *op cit;* pp. 68-69.
45. D.R. Patil, *op cit;* p. 91.
46. *Ibid*; p. 144.
47. BDG, gaya, p. 219 (Abbreviation BDG stands for Bihar District Gazetter).
48. The ruins on the hills were first noticed by R.D. Banerjee in 1906 with an additional note.

    See R.D. Banerjee and Bloch, *JPASB*; 1906. P. 77.
49. Buchanan, Shahabad, 79-81.
50. Buchanan, Patna-Gaya. I, pp. 142-44.
51. *Ibid.*
52. Broadley, JASB; 1872: p. 254.
53. H. Shastri, MASI; p. 66.
54. Buchanan. *Patna-Gaya*. I. Pp. 160-62.
55. *Ibid.*
56. D.R. Patil, op cit; p. 424.
57. Buchanan Report on Patna-Gaya, I, pp. 171-75.

    D.R. Patil, op. *Cit; p. 149.*
58. *Ibid.*
59. Buchanan Report on Patna-Gaya, I, pp. 171-75.

    D.R. Patil, *op. Cit;* p. 187.

60. R.L. Mitra, *Bodh Gaya* the Hermitage of Sakyamuni, p. 71.
61. D.R. Patil, *op. Cit;* p. 60.
62. J. Burgess, *Buddhist art in India,* p.1.
63. J. Burgess, *op. Cit.* P. 75.
64. *Ibid.*

Chapter IV

Development of Buddhism in the Time of Aśoka and the Later Mauryas (269 B.C.—188 B.C.)

Among the more romantic hypotheses regarding Aśoka's affiliation towards Buddhism, the one more interesting is that Kalinga war "transformed Aśoka's personality and perspective". From the Buddhist sources we learn that in the beginning Aśoka was not a Buddhist and for three years he paid honour to Pāśhanda infidels. He was paying attention to the Nigranthas (jainas), ājīvikas, Brāhmaṇas and other asceties and sects and used to make gifts to them. Aśoka maintained 60,000 Brāhmaṇas for three years as his father had done earlier. According to Dīpvamśa, Aśoka was converted to Buddhism three years after coronation. It is narrated that Aśoka was anxious to know the true path, and he invited members of all the religious orders to Pāṭalīputra, where the third Buddhist council was held, gave them costly presents and put questions to them.[1] None could answer satisfactorily and so all were killed by Aśoka, who began to search for an *arhat*.

That the Kalinga war transformed the ways and beliefs of Aśoka overnight is hard to accept. Modern historians like R.S. Sharma and Romila Thapar reject this notion due to its 'irrational' and 'unhistori-cal' interpretations. At some places Romila Thapar Mentions[2] that the 'change of heart' theory is rather based on fabrications of Buddhist chronicles who desire to show that before Aśoka' adopted Buddhism he was a cruel man who killed his ninety nine brothers and under the influence of Buddhism he became a votary of non-violence, tolerance.

Empirical scrutiny of the incident that after Kaliṅga war Aśoka's heart changed, he adopted Buddhism and denounced war does not stand the test of the time. The fact was that, (which have been corroborated by many modern historians) after Kaliṅga war there was no such major power as Kaliṅga that could be subdued by sword.

In this chapter it is intended to raise some basic controversies regarding Aśoka's conversion to Buddhism and what measures did he take to propagate this new religion in India and other neighbouring countries. Aśoka has, in many ways, been regarded as the representative of this age. To what extent this new religion suited the ruler and the society as well?

Not withstanding clear statements in the Ceylonese chornicles many scholars hold that Aśoka was converted to Buddhism some time after the Kaliṅga war fought in the 8th year of his coronation.[3] According to F. W. Thomas[4] "the slaughter and sufferings which attended the conquest (of Kaliṅga) produced upon his mind such an impression that it proved a turning point in his career. He joined the Buddhist order as a lay disciple, and thus subjected himself to the influence of ideas of which he was destined to be one of the greatest propagators". According to Bhandarkar[5] Aśoka became a Buddhist, a year after his conquest of Kaliṅga. Raychaudhuri[6] is also of the same view'.[7] "The sight of the misery and bloodshed in that sanguinary compaign made a deep impression on him and awakened in him great feeling of (anuśocanā) remorse, profound sorrow and regret." About this time he came under the influence of the Buddhist teaching. He rejected the view that Aśoka's conversion to Buddhism is to be placed before the Kalinga war, and held that his conversion took place a little less than one and a half years after his *abhiseka*, i.e. little less than one and a half years after the Kalinga war. According to him the supporters of the theory that Aśoka became a convert to Buddhism before the war have to explain "why a recent convert to Buddhism should engage in a sanguinary conflict involving the death of countless' śramanas."[8] A recent writer expresses the same idea; "The obvious doubt as regards the latter theory is whether as a recent convert to non-violent Buddhism, Aśoka could have engaged in such a largescale war.[9] D. R. Bhandarkar[10] states, "Aśoka become a Buddhist in the 9th year of his regin, that is, a year after his conquest of Kalinga." In Sastri's view[11] in the 11th year on account of his remorse at the thought of the incidents of the Kalinga war he adopted Buddhism as his creed."[12] According to Hultzsch[13] Aśoka became a Upāsaka in the 10th year of his reign. No serious consideration can be given to the view of H. C. Seth[14] that Aśoka became an ardent Buddhist during the last ten years of his reign. Fleet's view that Aśoka was converted to Buddhism in the 30th year of his reign is in clear contradiction to R. E. VIII.

However, the other view that Aśoka was converted to Buddhism before the Kalinga war in 265 B. C. has been held by Mookerji[15] and strongly defended by Eggermont[16] who on the basis of the critical study of MRE and R. E. XIII concludes that Aśoka was converted to Buddhism as a Upāsaka a few months before the Kalinga war at the end of Vassa of the 7th year of the reign. The R.E. XIII clearly states that in the 8th year of his coronation Kalinga was conquered, and thereafter Aśoka's observance of Dhamma, (*Dhammāpalana*) or *Dhammasilana*, love of *Dhamma* (*Dharma-Kāmanā*), and his preaching of the Dhamma (Dhamma anusaste) became intense (tivra).[17] It suggests that before this he was just an ordinary follower of Buddhism like others not zealous in the faith, and his conversion to Buddhism may be taken to be in about 266-265 B.C., as suggested by the Ceylonese Chornicles.[18] There is no incontrovertible evidence to reject the statement of the Ceylonese Chronicles that he was converted to Buddhism three years after his consecration by Nigrodha who was 7 years old. What might have happened is that Aśoka's search for an *Arhat* to show him the true path at which he would personally subscribe after he was disappointed by the Brāhmanas and other religious orders, might have made some Buddhist teacher to tutor Nigrodha a child of 7 years and a relative of Aśoka, in order to impress on Aśoka's mind the miraculous power the Buddhist teaching had. It would also help, after 7 years of the murder of his elder brother by Aśoka, in establishing a reconciliation between the uncle and the nephew, who later might have proved his disinterestedness in any future claim on the throne by becoming a monk. The Ceylonese chronicles[19] also specifically mention that Mogalliputta Tissa (Probably, identified with Upagupta of the Yuan Chawang's accounts) gave Pabbajā to Mahaendra and Samghamitrā at the age of 20 and 18 respectively. After Aśoka was consecrated for 6 years, i.e. 263 2 B.C. and thus Aśoka became a relative of the Faith. In the 4th year of his reign his brother Upraja Tissa was also given *Pabajjā* by *Mahadhammarakkhita.*[20] It is true that Aśoka waged the Kalinga war after he was converted to Buddhism. This may be indirectly supported by Taranatha[21] who says that on the advice of Yaśa at the palace of Aśoka, the latter paid honour to the Buddha and Samgha and then conquered the Nagas, and through the power of his merit earned by honouring the Buddha and 60,000 Arhats in the palace he conquered the whole of Jambudvipa south of the Vindhyas. Being a follower of Buddhism or jainism did not prevent any king before and after Aśoka in waging war. Mention may be made of Ajātasatru, Prasenjit, Udayana, Khāravela, Dharmapāla, Devapāla, and many others who in spite of being followers of religion of non-violence waged numerous bloody wars. Aśoka, who was every inch an imperialist till the Kalinga war did not mean change in Aśoka's religion, but sensitive Aśoka struck by the carnage in the war, began to introspect deeply and was spurred to zealous religious activities including active consideration to sanctity of life of men and animals. It is not certain when the *M.R.E.I.* was inscribed and the interpretation of 200,50,6 have not been unanimous. The *M.R.E.I.* Only states the stages in the growth of Aśoka's zeal towards religion. At first he was an indifferent Buddhist, a lay disciple, and then for the last more than one year had been zealously exerting for the promotion of the Dhamma. Now a question arises what event *spurred* him to exert for promotion of *Dhamma*? Mere conversion to Buddhism did not act as the spur. The Kaliṅga war was an epoch-making event, which made him announce a new foreign policy and led him to think of promotion of *Dhamma*. In the opinion of Bhandarkar[22] the empire of Magadha could have extended over whole of this country, making India one nation and afterwards also might have spread even beyond making Pataliputra, like Rome, the capital of the world. "But in the consequence of the foreign policy of *Dhamma-Vijaya* inaugurated by Aśoka, India was lost to nationalism and political greatness. Nevertheless she has doubtless gained in consmopolitanising humanity. The first important result of this might have been to go on a pilgrimage to *Sambodhi* in the 10th year of his conversion.[23] Sambodhi means the Bodhi-tree of Bodh-Gayā[24]. This pilgrimage may be connected with the tour for 256 nights mentioned by Aśoka in M.R.E. (Rupanath and Sahasram). It was after obtaining Enlightenment at Bodh-Gaya that the Buddha decided to preach his *Dhamma* and went to Sārnāth. It may be that with the pilgrimage to Bodh-Gaya, Aśoka set out on the propagation of his *Dhamma*.

There is no doubt that *Aśoka's personal religion was Buddhism to which he was converted from Brahmanism.* Doubt expressed by some scholars that Aśoka was not a Buddhist do not bear scrutiny. Heras[25] and Dikshitar's[26] arguments show that Aśoka'a faith was not Buddhist but Brāhmanism has been ably refuted by Gokhale.[27] The clear and emphatic testimony of the Ceylonese chronicles and Indian Buddhist literature that Aśoka was a Buddhist, and contributed much to the progress of Buddhism cannot be questioned without pointing to any unassailable evidence. If the Buddists only to exalt their position and religion, adopted falsely Aśoka as a Buddhist emperor, then why did they not claim many other great emperors of India like Chandragupta Maurya, Samudragupta or Chandragupta II as Buddhists? Of course there are certainly many romantic, miraculous and exaggerated accounts in the early Buddhist literature about Aśoka and his role in the promotion of Buddhism and the change that it brought in him but there is no reason to doubt that Aśoka was a Buddhist and Buddhism prospered much in his reign. The edicts of Aśoka prove this.[28] In the *MRE*—I, in the maski edition he calls himself *Buddha Sake*, and in the Rupanath edition. *Prakāśa śāke* i.e. he was a Buddhist openly a follower of Sakya i.e. he Buddha. In the same edict in Brahamagiri version he declares that he had been a lay disciple (Upāsaka) for more than 2 years and a half and a year ago he has visited the Samgha which definitely means Buddhist Saṃgha.[29] The Bhabru or Bairat No. 2 Rock edict[30] contains the salutation of Aśoka to the *Buddha, Dharma* and *Saṃgha* and he wishes the Saṃgha—the Buddhist order all health and happiness. In this edict Aśoka cites passages from the Buddhist scriptures which have been shown to have been taken from the well known Buddhist sacred works. The phrase occurring in the edict, Whatsoever has been said by the Lord Buddha, all that has been well said has been identified with a passage in the *Aṅguttra Nikāya*. It has been well pointed out that the code of conduct prescribed by the Buddha in the *Ratha Vinita Sutta, Nalaka Sutta, Mahā Aṅiyavamsa and Tavatak-sutta* as stated by Bhddhaghosa in his *Viśuddhimagga* may be in almost identical words be recognised in this edict of Aśoka, 'What Buddhaghosa therefore selected as the most important and representative texts for a *Bhiksu* might well have been cited by Aśoka too.[31] Aśoka's anxiety for the prosperity of the Buddhist church, and for the proper religious conduct of monks according to Buddha's prescripts certainly would be out of place if he was not a Bhddhist himself. From the *R.E.* ; VIII we learn that after 10 years of his coronation, he visited, *Sambodhi*

(Both-Gaya).[32] The Rummindei inscription informs us that he visited Lumbini after 20 years of his coronation, and here he offered worship, erected a stone pillar and reduced the land tax (*Bhāga*) from 1/6 to 1/8[33]. He also in the same year revisited Nigliva where he had in the 15th year after his coronation enlarged the stupa of *Kanakamuni.*[34] In Kalsi rock where a copy of the 14 Rock Edicts has been found, there is a picture of an elephant, below which 'gajotame' is inscribed. in Dhauli also the above inscription is on a rock-cut figure of a large elephant and the work 'Seto' i.e. 'Sweta' is inscribed, suggesting white elephant. In the Girnar 13th Rock edicts also the words meaning white elephant, giver of happiness to all (*Śvetohasti Sarvalokasukha Kārināma*) are engraved. Elephant is also sculptured in the famous Lion capital of Aśoka found at Sarnath. White Elephant represents Buddha who is traditionallty believed to have entered his mother's womb in the form of a white elephant in the dream of Maya.[35] In the pillar edict—VII in which Aśoka says that the *Dharmamahāmātras* are employed among all sects, he immediately after, specifically mentions the Samgha (Buddhist Church), as distinguished from other sects or churches, in whose business also by his order the *Dharmamahāmātras* were to be employed. The use of the word '*Samghathasi*' (Interest of the Samgha) may suggest special interest in the Buddhist Church as opposed to other sects by Aśoka. Abolition and /or restriction of killing of animals or birds, on particular pious dates, which are pious for the Buddhist (P.E.,V) may also betray his Buddhist faith. These authentic epigraphic evidences indicating that Aśoka was a Buddhist are strongly supplemented by the Buddhist literatures Ceylonese, India, Chinese and Tibetan. Both the *Mahāvamśa* and the *Dīpavmśa* speak of conversion of Aśoka to Buddhism and setting up of stupas and monasteries by him. The *Dīvyāvadāna* and *Aśokāvadāna* relate many incidents of Aśoka's carrier as a Buddhist. Huen Tsang refers to Aśoka being a Buddhist and patronising Buddhism. Tibetan historian Tārānātha alludes to Aśoka's many activities as a Buddhist.[36]

That Aśoka's personal religion was Buddhism may now be accepted as certain. By the time Aśoka ascended the throne, there were many religions prevalent in Magadha—Brahmanism, Jainism, Ājīvikism, Buddhism and many other sects (P.E. Vii).[37] According to the Buddhist literature Aśoka was converted to Buddhism from Brahmanism by Nigrodha, and established in Theravāda by Moggaliputra Tissa. Without giving any credence to the role miracles in convincing Aśoka of the superiority of Buddhism over other sects, or to the alleged unseemly behaviour of the Brāhmaṇa and other priests on the occasion of receiving gifts by Aśoka there must be some, deeper reasons why Aśoka deliberately chose Buddhism as his personal religion. There is no doubt *that the questioning spirit, which dominated religions and intellectual life in the 6th century B.C. and resulted in the rise of numerous non-Brāhmanical or anti-Brāhmanical religions, continued in the early Maurya period.* Kautilya's *Arthaśāstra*[38] speaks of Ājīvikas, Sākya (Buddhist) and other non-orthodox sects and suggests measures to combat young men and women joining this religious and spiritual quest abandoning responsibilities of domestic life. *Buddhism has not by his time become that great religion which it was certainly during the time of Aśoka and after his death.* The Mauryan kings were not particularly wedded to orthodox Brāhmanism. Though Candragupta was very much guided by Kautilya, the champion of orthodox Brāhmanism, he appears to have in later year embraced Jainism.[39] Bindusāar's queen was very much influenced by the Ājīvika monk,[40] and Aśoka himself and his grandson Daśaratha made gifts including rock-cut caves to them in Barabar-Nagarjuni hills in Magadha.[41] Therefore, it is quite reasonable to presume that Aśoka was very much accquainted with the currents of religious thoughts and propaganda. His edicts breathe his sensitiveness, his introspective habit, his practical approach to do good to the people and above all his anxiety to follow a righteous path. This must have made him to study and discuss various religious path. This must have made him to study and discuss various religious doctrines and practices, their mutual differences and varying emphasis and to make an attempt to find out which of these would answer most satisfactorily the craving of his soul and provide him with the best psychological and spiritual base to win the hearts of his people and help him in realising his practical ambition to promote welfare of the whole world (sarvalokahitāya).[42] From the Ceylonese Chronicles[43] we learn that he had called an assembly of monks or priests of various religious orders and when he was disappointed by them he found satisfaction in the principles of Buddhism, which was at that time a simple religion with emphasic on good conduct in words, thought and deed, and afforded the rational basis of its philosophy and was intensely humane in spirit.[44] Narrow sectarian beliefs, blind superstitions, worship of innumerable gods and goddesses, and practice of extensive asceticism being part and parcel of many other prevalent religions with numerous rituals and practices, some very unseemly and grossly irrational, could not be accepted by Aśoka who, as we know, viewed religion as an integral number, a powerful force in maintaining stability, and promoting all round progress in the far flung empire inhabited by peoples of differing social, intellectual, spiritual, and moral standards. Buddhism with its emphasis on ethical principles, proper social norms, rational philosophy, human principles and confidence in capacity of any individual to reach highest state of *Arhatship* very much appealed not only to the sensitive and introspective Aśoka as a man but to Aśoka the emperor well alive to his sense of responsibility to give stability and to maintain peace and progress in the far flung empire.

Though Aśoka became a Buddhist, and a zealous Buddhist, it would be wrong to suggest that he became a monk. In the MRE, I Aśoka uses the word *Saṁgha* Upayi (te) or *Upete* or *Upayate* or *Upagate.*[45] This is supposed to mean that he became a monk or joined the monk's order. It should really mean that for more than two years and a half he was a lay disciples (Upāsaka) and had not exerted well but since more than a year he visited the Saṁgha, he exerted greatly. As a matter of fact all the edicts of Aśoka breathe the spirit of an emperor very much alive to his regal sense of duty and responsibility and they certainly do not suggest at all the parching of a high priest for converting non-believers to his faith. It is impossible to describe his activity, as Smith[46] has gone, "as not so much that of pious emperor as of an archbishop, possessed of exceptional temporal power. Similarly there is no basis to substantiate the story in the *Divyāvadāna* that Aśoka towards the end of his life renounced the empire and turned a monk.[47] P.E. VII, was issued in the 27th year when Aśoka was very much a king and the statement in M.R.E., I *Saṃghaupate* does not mean that Aśokā became a monk, and there is no evidence in early Indian Buddhism that a monk combined in himself the role and title of the king.

Though Aśoka did not take the monk's robe, he certainly contributed to the promotion of Buddhism and in strengthening the unity in the Buddhist church. We have already seen that he enlarged the stūpa of *Kanakamuni,* a former Buddha. He also *enforced* unity in the church and proclaimed punishment for such Buddhists who promoted schism in the church. He declared, "No one is to cause dissension in the order. The order of monks and nuns has been united and thus unity should last far as long as my sons and great grandsons and the moon and the sun. Whoever creates a schism in the order, whether monk or nun, is to be dressed in white garments and to be put in a place not inhabited by monks or nuns.[48] Aśoka was not only content with issuing the royal proclamation to the monks or nuns of the *Saṁgha,* but he asked the laymen to come on every *uposatha* day and endorse this order. He directs the officers *(Mahāmātras)* of the state to regularly attend the *uposatha* and endorse this order and make it known (i.e. give wide publicity). Throughout their jurisdiction they had to circulate this exactly according to the text of the proclamation. Of course this edict is a clear proof of the Buddhist king Aśoka exercising royal authority to maintain unity in the Buddhist church. This action might have been also influenced by political consideration. Aśoka the king of Magadha, could not break with impunity the risk to peace and progress which would be threatened by violent disputations amongst the Buddhists who constituted a large population and wielded large and organised influence in Magadha—the nerve centre of the empire. However, Aśoka's interest in the unity and prosperity of the Buddhist samgha cannot be ignored. It may be true that Aśoka's proclamations about restriction or absolute prohibition of killing of animals, and his humanitarian programme of providing hospitals for men and animals, for building of roads with trees and rest-houses on the road-sides, and of promotion of ethical and rational values were somewhat inspired by his devotion to Buddhism but nothing specifically Buddhist, such as the four noble truths, *Nirvāna,* the Midddle path and Buddha's other sayings are traceable in the general edicts like the 14 Rock edicts, 7 pillar Edicts, and Kalinga Edicts.

But Buddhist literary traditions speak much more about Aśoka's activities towards the promotion of Buddhism. We are told that *Devānāmpriya*[49] of Ceylon became a Buddhist on the advice and persuasion of Aśoka. Ceylonese chronicles[50] say that Aśoka's son Mehendra and daughter Saṅghamitrā born of Devi of Vidisā went to Ceylon one after another to convert the king, the queen, the officers and servants and subjects of Ceylon. R.E. II and R.E. XIII mention *Tāmraparni*[51] i.e., Ceylon amongst other foreign and border kingdoms where Aśoka's welfare schemes and propagation of *Dhamma* were introduced, but of course as was natural, Aśoka does not specifically refer to Buddhism and its promotion in this as in other general edicts. It appears that Aśoka was careful in not mixing himself and his royal authority and public welfare programmes with actual Buddhist missionary activities.

Aśoka was for both religious and political reasons anxious to see that unity in the large and influential Buddhist church is maintained; while this was natural for a Buddhist to hope, for a king over peoples of diverse religious beliefs it was still more necessary to see that the occasions for violent disputes are reduced. Ceylonese chronicles inform us that 236 years after Nirvāna of the Buddha (486-236-250 B.C.) many followers of other sects such as Pāndurangas, Jatilas, Nirgranthas, Acelakas, and others had entered the Aśokārāma at Pātaliputra with the Buddhists.[52] Probably this was in pursuance of Aśoka's policy of members of different religious sects discussing together their irreligious principles, and thereby come to appreciate each other's religious views.[53] But according to the Buddhist sources, this was not relished by orthodox Buddhists of the Vinaya school, who found many rules of discipline and procedure neglected or relaxed. It is declared that "Ājivikas and sectarians of different descriptions ruined the Doctrine[54] we are informed that as the income of the samgha went on increasing with new converts, many hereties became monks (put on yellow robe) and they proclaimed their own doctrines as that of the Buddha. This made the orthodox monks suspend the practice of *Uposatha* and *Pavāarnā* ceremonies for as many as seven years.[55] The MV[56] informs us that a royal minister used to watch the interest of the Samgha. Probably he was to see that the king's religious policy of *Samavāya* and mutual religious discussions in peace is followed. *R.E; V.* probably refers to this special interest of the king in the Samgha, who deputed *Mahāmātras* to look after the Samgha; and it appears that in the *Aśokārāma* in the capital, Aśoka's policy of members of different sects discussing mutual religious principles was being experimented. The orthodox Buddhist monks did not like that the rigid rules of discipline be not followed by others. It is certain that among the Buddhist monks themselves there were many who did not subscribe to rigid *Vinaya* rules as insisted upon by the orthodox priests, they there upon did not perform the *Uposatha* ceremony. This was very serious and the minister informed the king and asked his instruction. The king appears to be anxious to maintain both peace and mixed assemblage of monks in the monastery and ordered his officer to see that *Uposatha* is performed in the *Aśokārāma*. The minister tactlessly while proclaiming the orders of the king, wanted the recalcitrant orthodox priests to perform *Uposatha* under the threat of physical force. Fanatic priests refused and many were killed. Priest Tissa, a younger brother of the king, took their side and was ready to die for the maintenance of the orthodox rules. The unnerved minister reported the serious situation to the king, who came repented and wanted to know if there was some wise monk who would show the right path and end controversies.[57] While the details of the story may be rightly doubted, there is no doubt that there were schisms in the Buddhist church, and that Aśoka's policy of promotion of religious peace by encouraging monk of different religions or sectarian views to live together, discuss, mutually respond to each other's religion, and develop a spirit of religious toleration was not an undiluted success. In the *Divyāvadāna* there is a reference to riots in Puṇḍravardhana and Pāṭaliputra instigated by Brāhmaṇas and Aśoka's brother Vītāśoka was killed by mistake. Many Brāhmaṇās also were killed. In the Chinese translation of the Asokāyadana the riot led to massacre of the Nigranthas and Aśoka's brother also mistaken to be a Nigrantha was killed.[58]

However, Moggaliputra Tissa was invited and he purged the heretics and accepted only such Buddhist monks as true Bhiksus who accepted the *Vibhajjā* doctrine.[59] That there was schism in the Buddhist church and royal authority was invited to punish the non-conformists is clear from the Sārnāth pillar Edict.

After restoring the purity of the Buddhist order in the *Aśokārāma*, the third Buddhist council was held at Pāṭaliputra under the presidentship of Moggaliputra Tissa. The council finally settled the rules of discipline and Moggliputra composed the *Kathāvatthu*. However, the 'historicity of the council under the patronage of Aśoka remains *doubtful*, 'though the *M. V.* clearly states that under the auspices of king Aśoka in his *17th* year of reign (252 B.C.) this convocation on religion was brought to a close in nine months.[60] There is no reference to the council in Aśoka's inscriptions. The Mahāyānist texts do not refer to this, Eggermont[61] has argued that even if the council was held and schism in the Buddhist church was purged and schism *Edicts* were proclaimed, this should have happened after the 28th year of Aśoka's reign. According to the Ceylonese chronicles the third council was held in the 17th years of Aśoka's reign. The schism Edict might have been issued after the purge in the *Aśokārāma* by Moggaliputra and Aśoka thereafter anxious to maintain peace in the Saṁgha particularly in Pāṭaliputra.

Among many other religious sects of Aśoka the chief may be regarded as the building of Stupas and *Sanghārāmas*. He is reputed to have built as many as 84,000 stupas[62] which may be a convenient hyperbole but is quite evident that he did built quite a good number of them. For Huien Tsang mentions several he had seen at many places in India as far as Puṣkalāvati.[63] He is also supposed to have distributed the relics of the Buddha in quite different ways than was done after the death of the Buddha[64] and was responsible for despatching a branch of the Bodhi tree to Ceylon with his daughter Sanghamitrā.[65] To his mission we have already referred. Thus under the loving enthusiasm of Aśoka the Buddhist faith predominated all other faiths in the 3rd century B.C.[66]

After the death of Aśoka the Saṁgha was split up into different sects. About the religious policy of the successors of Aśoka we do not know excepting his grandson Daśaratha who seems to have carried on his grandfather's policy of religious toleration by donating some caves to the Ājīvikas.[67] But this period was one of localisation and decentralisation of the Buddhist monastic institutions which was accelerated by the anti-Buddhist policy of Puśyamitra Suṅga.[68] His successors, however, did not follow his policy[69] as is evidenced by the sculptures of Barhut and Saṁchi during their reign.[70] But the Buddhist church as a body hardly revived after the blow struck at it by Puśyamitra.

The main burden of Buddhism was centred on equality and synthesis. In the political sphere, this synthesising tendency reached its highest point in the reign of Aśoka. It may be true that the policy of *dhammavijaya* led to disastrous national results as has been claimed.[71] But it must also be pointed out that the real cause of the downfall of the Mauryas lies in this that the successors of Aśoka were too weak and powerless to maintain a strong centre against the disintegrating parts. To oversimplify the matter— the forces of disintegration outweighed and outran the forces of synthesis. The very fact that Aśoka had to fight only one war speaks of a peaceful and undisturbed reign. But the crux of the problem lies in Aśoka's over emphasis on the religious rather than the social aspect of Buddhism. He adopted the faith of the Buddha and with it a certain amount of zeal, but the monarch turned a "monk", a preacher, which produced disastrous results. At the same time the process of synthesis had comparatively less time and support at its disposal than the forces of Brāhmanism. Buddhism as a social, and religious force had only 200 years to develop at its disposal. And a social movement opposed by a multitude of hostile forces can hardly show any result in such a short time.

Likewise here in the king's territory, among the Yonas and Kambojas, among the Nabhakas and Nabhities, among the Bhojas and Piṭinikas, among the Andhras and Palidass— everywhere (people) are conforming to *Devānāmpriya's* instruction in morality.[72] According to this epigraph Aśoka was responsible for the spread of Buddhism all over India and the adjacent territories. What happened to his missions beyond the borders of India we are not in a position to say. Again whether they were religious missions or *good-will missions* is also not clear. It is highly probable that they were of the latter variety and must have carried out Aśoka's programme of ministering to the medical needs of the people. That the effect was not wholly negative in religious matters can easily be deduced from the influence of Buddhist ideas on the Christian religion.

Almost all prominent scholars like Smith,[73] Bhandarkar,[74] and Mookherji,[75] are in agreement regarding the authenticity of Aśokan missions. But Rhys Davids[76] is sceptical about them and calls them mere "royal rhodomontade." He believes that a highly civilized people like the Greeks were not likely to receive favourably the 'barbarian' missionaries and learn anything from them. Bhandarkar has very ably refuted this view and clearly shown that there was nothing impossible in such a mission.[77] Aśoka spread Buddhism as far as Northern Bengal, Nepal, Kashmir, Gandhara, Kamboja, Saurastra and Tāmraparṇi, thus transforming a small sect into a religion of considerable importance.[78] In Aśoka's reign Buddhist missionaries made strong efforts to penetrate into Bengal[79] and Andhra,[80] and eventually the faith was strongly established in Northern India.[81]

In order to understand clearly the process of expansion undergone by Buddhism in the reign of Aśoka it is necessary to examine the Aśoka claim as well as the priestly list.

THE BUDDHIST COUNCILS

Apart from the missions with which we dealt earlier another important occurrence in the ecclesiastical history of Buddhism has the name of Aśoka associated with it. We are told by the *Mahāvaṁśa* that encouraged by the bountiful gifts of the generous Aśoka many heretics entered the Buddhist fold who could not be controlled according to the vinaya rules and as a consequence for seven years the *uposatha* ceremony could not be held. Eventually the heretics were expelled and an assembly of learned monks was held at Pāṭaliputra to fix the doctrine and discipline of the Master.[82] This event took place in the 17th regional year of Aśoka.[83]

This was the third council, according to the Buddhist chronicles to be held for the settlement of disputed problems.

The first was held immediately after the death of Buddha, the second a 150 years thereafter and the third during the reign of Aśoka. As we are mainly concerned with the development of Buddhism as a religion with special reference to the position of the laity therein we deferred discussion on these till now. An attempt will now be made to assess the historical value of these councils and the part the laity played therein.

THE FIRST COUNCIL

Immediately after the death of the Buddha fissiparous tendencies in the *Saṁgha* began to manifest themselves in the utterances of monks like subhead who openly admitted that he was happy at the Buddha's death, that he could now act as he liked without anybody remonstrating him. Then Mahakassapa invited the leading monks saying "come sirs, let us chant together the Dhamma and the Vinaya before what is not dhamma is spread abroad and what is dhamma is put aside; before what is not vinaya is spread abroad and what is vinaya is put aside."[84] Then 499 arahats were called and Ananda was included when he became an arahat. Upali was responsible for Vinaya and Ananda for the dhamma and the sayings of the Buddha were put into some shape at *Rājagha* under the patronage of Ajātaśatru. This, in short, is the story of the 1st council. It has been criticised in diverse ways and its historicity questioned. Oldenberg first seriously questioned the authentic nature of this tradition and called it "pure invention, and, moreover, an invention of very ancient date.[85] Rhys Davids[86] analyses the passage concerning subhadda in the *Mahāparinibbāna Sutta* and comes to the conclusion that "the last two paragraphs in the *Dīgha Nikāya* are transposed in the Vinaya.[87] The Vinaya account coupled with the silence of the Dīgha Sutta does compel one to look with suspicion at the authenticity of the 1st council. But as against this discrepancy we have corroborative evidence from the Northern Buddhist sources. The Tibetan book, "Life of Buddha"[88] for instance, contains an account of the 1st council of Magadha with only slight modifications. The motive mentioned in the cullavagga i.e. to recite the Dhamma and the Vinaya, is easy to believe but the story of Subhadda is clearly an interpolation as the former motive though quite sufficient in itself has, without the Subhadda episode, none of the qualities of a dramatic occurrence. Even admitting the discrepancies pointed out by Oldenberg it is not difficult to hold that the tradition of the 1st council has a firm historical foundation.[89] It is by no means "incredible" states Kern[90] that the disciples after the death of the founder of their sect came together to come to an agreement concerning the principal points of the creed and of discipline. Rhys Davids[91], Geiger,[92] Majumdar,[93] are of similar opinion.

THE SECOND COUNCIL

A hundred and fifty years after the 1st council at Rājaghra came off the second council at Vaiśāli. The circumstances surrounding it were more turbulent than the previous one. The Vajjian monks, it appears, promulgated the "ten points"[94] regarding disciplinary matters which were resented by Yāsa who rebuked them for doing something against rules. Yāsa referred this matter to Sambhuta Sanavasa, an aged Bhikkhu, and asked for his opinion. An assembly was called for the purpose of deciding the propriety or otherwise of these "points."

The assembly met and gave their ruling against these "ten points." That is, to put it very briefly, the story of the 2nd council. It is corroborated by northern tradition[95] and is generally accepted as true.[96] It also, like the first involves us into certain discrepancies like the age of certain old monks therein which would be as a hundred and sixty etc. But it certainly has historical basis as is accepted by all well known authorities.[97]

THE THIRD COUNCIL

According to the Mahāvaṁśa the third council was held at Pāṭaliputra in the 17th regnal year of Aśoka. The immediate reason for convening the council , according to the same authority, was that tempted by the generous treatment accorded to the Saṁgha many heretics entered the Saṁgha and consequently the Saṁgha being impure the *uposatha* could not be held. Aśoka came to know of it and ordered that uposatha should immediately be held. A minister of his bungled the task and there was a considerable slaughter of monks, at which the king was much perturbed.

After this event the Saṁgha was purged and under the presidentship of Moggaliputta Tissa, who composed the *Kathāvatthu,* the 3rd assembly was held. This account is full of the usual contradictions and difficulties. How, for instance, is it possible, that the heretics remained undetected in the Saṁgha for seven years? We find no corroboration for this assembly from the northern tradition. Aśoka in his edicts does not refer to such an assembly. If an important ecclesiastical matter like an assembly of monks had taken place Aśoka would certainly have made a mention of it in his Saṁgha edict.

The Pali books, again, speak of the 18 schools but Aśoka, wherever he has occasion, refers to the fraternity as the Saṁgha, meaning thereby the Saṁgha[98] of the four quarters and not of any particular denomination. From this it may be presumed that Aśoka did not know of any sects. But then how are we to reconcile the Pali claim that the schism occurred at the second council and sects started appearing before the time of Aśoka? If we accept the Pali claim[99] that sects were in existence before Aśoka's time then we may agree with Kern that the third council of Pāaliputra was a part meeting of the Vibhajjavadis,[100] in an attempt to reconcile these contradictions Bhandarkar[101] and Mookerji have suggested that the 2nd council really came off in the reigh of Aśoka and not earlier as claimed by the Ceylon chronicles. Mookerji[102] further adds that the edict was addressed to the council. Treading on the same ground of epigraphic evidence we can hold that Aśoka does not know of the sects then in that case the second council must have been held in the last years of Aśoka's reign[103] and the sects sprang up thereafter.

The 150 years after Buddha attributed to the Vaiśālī council looks a suspicious figure and so are the details. Aśoka's warning regarding the stern action to be taken against those who bring about a split in the Saṁgha indicates the first attempt and evidently the 2nd council. The 3rd council must have been held either in the reign of Daśarath, Aśoka's grandson or his successors who nominally ruled over Magadha from Pāaliputra before the advent of the Śuṅgas and hence must have been purely a party affair.

The Brāhmaṇical reaction which set in shortly after the death of Aśoka was brought to culmination and fruition by the rise of Puśyamitra to the throne of Magadha.[104] The *Mānavadharmaśāstra* visibly śmymbolises this political revolution.[105] The Brāhmaṇical counter-movement[106] epitomised in the rule of Puśyamitra saw, first of all, a Brāhmana installed on the royal throne. This brought the Brāhmaṇa reaction to the forefront and consequently all those practices stopped by Aśoka were revived. Puśyamitra performed the Aśvamedha in the same Pāṭaliputra from where Aśoka issued the order forbidding all sacrifices.[107] These sacrifices may have helped him to acquire the status of a king and make the people forget that he was a usurper.[108] The *Divyāvadāna* mentions a tradition that Puśyamitra persecuted the Buddhists and we see no reason for doubting the statement.[109]

The Buddhist position, as regards the division of society on cast basis is clear and uncompromising. Buddhism we have remarked earlier started as a "Protestant" monastic movement. Its nature was two-fold. The first part embodied the rationalistic aspect which assumed the nature of the repudiation of the authority of the sacrificial ritualism attended by a meaningless slaughter of large numbers of animals. The revolt against the Brāhmanic theory of caste also falls in this part. The second part consists of the synthetic spirit of the Buddhist monastic movement which was a logical conclusion of its first aspect. N.K. Dutt[110] pertinently points out that Buddhism was a protest against "the imposition of Brāhmanical belief and institutions upon a not very willing people, conquered but not vanquished." Buddhism spread with surprising rapidity throughout Magdha consequent upon its becoming a religion. This development has been fully traced in the first part of this work. In Aśoka Buddhism found the most valuable follower for he, by his royal support, made it a "state" religion and thus directly helped its outward spread. But with the advent of the śuṅgas and with them the resurgence of Brāhmaṇism in a militant attitude the tide had turned. The Śuṅgas, at least the first Śuṅga, reversed whatever Aśoka stood for. He performed the horse-sacrifices and it must have been in the nature of his policy that he advocated the theory of caste with redoubled vigour. Bhupendranath Dutta in an article "Brāhmaṇical counter revolution"[111] has exhaustively shown how the *Manu Smrti* breathes class-hatred throughout its pages and its venom is specially directed against the Buddhists who are indicted as Śūdras by Manu. The epithet may have been given on account of the liberal attitude of the Buddhist movement especially its repudiation of the theory of caste. The Viṣṇu Smrti[112] makes a king a protector of castes and Manu[113] clearly upholds a political revaluation which was also a social reaction. With what vigour the social reaction must have descended upon the people can easily be judged from Manu's attitude towards the other castes.

He, for instance, condemns association by Brāhmaṇas with non-Brāhmaṇas.[114] He exhorts the king to protect those who live as Āryas[115] evidently meaning thereby those who are in full sympathy with the social aspect of Brāhmaṇism. He calls the non-Āryans who pretend to be Āryas as 'Thorns (in the side of a people).'[116] The *Arthaśāstra* also advocates respectful treatment to the Brāhmaṇas. Those who perform sacrifices, spiritual guides, priests and those learned in the Vedas are to be granted *Brahmadeyya lands* yielding sufficient produce and exempted from taxes and fine.[117] But it is respect due to learning and spiritual duty and not due to class affiliations. The code of Manu, on the other hand, exhorts the people to respect a Brāhmaṇa because he is born a Brāhmaṇa, and as such he is *Bhudeva* (god on earth).

REFERENCE

1. See for details, R. *Thapar, Aśoka and Decline of the Mauryas, pp. 28-35.*
2. *Ibid.* p. 36.
3. R. Thapar, *op.cit;* p. 37.
4. *C. H. I.* pp. 495-96.
5. D.R. Bhandarkar, *Aśoka,* pp. 68-69.
6. *PHAI*; 6th Ed. p. 324.
7. H.C. Ray Chaudhuri, *Political History of Ancient India,* p. 108.
8. *PHAI; op. cit.* p. 325, note 1.
9. R. Thapar; *op. cit.*, p. 33.
10. Bhandarkar, D.R. *Camb. Hist. of India,* Vol. II. p. 30.
11. Sastri KBN—*Age of the Nandas and Mauryas,* p. 211.
12. Romila Thapar, op. cit. p. 35.
13. *C.I.I.* , Vol. I. p. XLVI.
14. *J.I.H.*,XVII, pp. 279 ff.
15. Mookerji, *Aśoka,* p. 23.
16. Eggermont, *Chronology, of the reign of Aśoka maurya.* p. 75.
17. The question of the conversion can be classified by referring to the edicts of Aśoka. The Minar Rock Edict is often regarded as his confession to belonging to the Buddhist faith. The relevant portion of his edicts reads,

    '... I have been a Buddhist layman for more than two and a half years but for a year I did not make much progress. Now for more than a year I have drawn close to the community of monks and have became more ardent....,

R. Thapar, *op.cit.* p. 37.

18. *Ibid,* p. 38.
19. D.V. VII p. 14-20; MV (Geiger) V. 209.
20. *M.V.* (Geiger) V. 160-172.
21. Schiefner, pp. 31-33 qu. Eggermont p. 88.
22. *Camb. Hist.* of *India*; Vol. II, p. 41.
23. *R.E.* VIII. According to Thapar, relying on Basham's interpretation the edicts are issued in the expired years as proved by the Kandhar inscription (Thapar *op. Cit;* p. 32). However D.C. Sircer (select Inscriptions, Vol. I. appendix-I pp. 527-28)in his Prakritised and Sanskritised versions of the Greek and Aramaric texts uses the same expression 'dasvasabh itena' as in other inscription of Aśoka, Mookerji's point that 25 deliveries were made in 26th year of his consecration prove that years (Aśoka p. 184) still holds the field.
24. Bhandarkar-*Aśoka*; p. 294, DV, XVI; Eggermont *op. cit,* p. 80.
25. *QJMS*; XVII. pp. 255 ff.
26. *Mauryan Polity*; pp. 276 ff.
27. Gokhale, B.G., *Buddhism and Aśoka*; pp. 69-71.
28. Detailed study of Aśokan edicts has been brought in R. Thapar, *op. cit;* pp. 34-35.
29. Brahmagiri Minor Rock Edict. Block, *Less Inscriptions* d' Aśoka; pp. 145-46.

    Vide, R. Thapar; *op. Cit.*; p. 36.
30. R. Thapar, *op. cit.*; p. 37.

    A far more direct avowal of Buddhist teaching is made in the Bhabru Edict. Unfortunately it is not dated, but we believe it to belong to the latter period of his region, issued perhaps at about the same time as the schism Edict. In the Bhabru Edict he states his acceptance of the Bhddhist creed, the faith in the Buddha and the saṁgha... and this Edict belongs to his personal religious manifestations.

31. Mookerji, *Aśoka*; p. 199 note.
32. Nikam, K.A. and Mekeon R. *The Edicts of Aśoka*; p. 227.
33. *Ibid.*
34. *Ibid, p.* 230.
35. Basham, A.L. *The wonder That was India*; p. 89.
36. Tārānāth, *The Chronology of the Reign of Aśoka*; p. 88.
37. The Sārnāth Pillar Edict speaks at one place that reads as follows... The rajukas (rural officers) are appointed over many hundreds of thousands of people; I have instructed them duly to encourage those people deveted to Dhamma..."

    R. Thapar, *op.cit.;* p. 265.
38. K.A.; III. 20, 16.
39. Parisishtaparvan; VIII, pp. 415 ff. LXXI.
40. R. Thapar, op. cit., p. 26.
41. Moorkerji, op. cit., pp. 205—208.
42. Kosambi, D.D. Introduction to the study of Indian History; p. 139.
43. DV; VI. 27—29.
44. Kosambi, D.D. op. cit; p. 139.
45. Thapar, R. op. cit; p. 263.
46. Smith, V.A., Aśoka; p. 356.
47. JRPS; 1913,p. 637.
48. Sārnāth Pillar Edict.
49. DV; XII, 1-7.
50. Ibid; VI, 15-17.
51. W. Geiger is not sure that Tāmraparṇi means Ceylon (MV; pp. XVII-XVIII).
52. *DV;* VII. 27-35.
53. *R.E.*; XII.
54. *DV;* VII. 38; *MV*; p. 26.
55. *MV*; (Geiger) V. 228—235 (Turnour).

56. *MV;* p. 27.
57. *MV*; pp. 25-27.
58. Qu. in Eggermont *op.cit*; p. III.113
59. *MV*; p. 27-28, Sārnāth pillar Edict.
60. MV; Geiger, V. 280-281. In the 17th year of kings reign 252 B.C.
61. Eggermont; op. cit, 116-119.
62. Beal, S. Buddhist Records of the Western world from the Chinese of Hiuen Tsang; I. pp. 109-110.
63. Beal, op. cit; II. p. 26.
64. Geiger, Mahāvaṁśa (tr.); p. 124.
65. Bhandarkar, *Aśoka;* p. 167.
66. *Ibid.*
67. Barabar Cave Inscription

    Also see, B.G. Gokhale, *Buddhism and Aśoka*; p. 91.
68. Marshall Faucher, *The Monuments of Sānchi;* I, p. 3.
69. *Ibid;* p. 3.
70. Barua & Sinha, *Barhut Inscription;* p. 1.
71. Several modern historians attributed this fact as the cause of the downfall of the Maurya empire.

    R. Thapar, *op. cit*; p. 40.
72. Hultzsch. *Inscriptions of Aśoka;* p. 170.
73. Mookerji, Aśoka. p. 46.
74. *Ibid*; p. 157.
75. *Ibid*; p. 77.
76. *Buddhist India*; pp. 298-99.
77. Bhandarkar, *op. cit*; p. 158.
78. Law, *N.I.A.*; III. p. 695.
79. *J.J.H.* ; XVII, p. 29.
80. B.C. Law Commemoration Volume, p. 346.
81. Law, *op. cit;* p. 696.

82. Geiger, *Mahāvaṁśa*; (Tr.). p. 49.

83. *Ibid*; p. 50.

84. Rhys Davids & Oldenberg, *Cullavagga*; XI, 1,2, *S.B.E;* XX, p. 372.

85. Oldenberg, Vinaya Texts; Vol. I, pp. XXI ff.

86. Rhys Davids, *Dialogues of Buddha*; II p. 77.

87. *Ibid;* p. 75.

88. Rockhill, *Life of Buddha*; pp. 150 ff.

89. *Z.D.M.G.*; 1898. p. 614.

90. Kern, *Manual of Indian Buddhism*; p. 103.

91. *Dial of Buddha;* II, p. 76.

92. *Mahāvaṁśa;* (tr.) p. LVII.

93. Law B.C., *Buddhistic studies; p. 43.*

94. Rhys Davids & Oldenberg, *Cullavagga*; XII, I, i, *S.B.E;* XX, p. 386.

95. Rockhill, *Life of Buddha*; pp. 178-179.

96. Of Geiger, Mahāvaṁśa; p. LXII & Kern, Manual of Indian Buddhism; p. 109.

97. Oldenberg, *Vinya pitaka;* p. XXIX, also Majumdar, *Buddhistic Studies.* P. 61.

98. Bhandarkar, Aśoka; p. 95 also Mookerji, *Aśoka;* p. 67.

99. E.G. Geiger, *Mahāvaṁśa* (tr.). p. LXII. The Tibetan "Life of the Buddha" but the account is confusing and unreliable.

See Rockhill, *op. cit.* p. 187.

100. Kern, *Manual of Buddhism*; p. 11.

101. Bhandarkar, *Aśoka;* p. 96.

102. Mookerji, *Aśoka;* p. 38.

103. *Ibid;* Men & Thought, p. 134.

104. Jayaswal, *Manu & Yājñyavalkya;* pp. 210, 230, 242; *Hindu Polity;* p. 156.

105. *Ibid*; XXIII.

106. *J.B.O.R.S.* XXIII, p. 255; also Ghosh in Law Commemoration Vol. p. 215.

107. Girnar, *R.E.* I.

108. Beni Prasad, *State in Ancient India*; p. 217.

109. Cf. Ghosh in law Commemoration Vol. pp. 215-16.

110. N.K. Dutt. *The Aryanisation of India*; p. 93.

111. *J.B.O. R.S.*; XXVI, pp. 263-78.

112. *Vaiṣṇava Dharmasastra;* III, 3.

113. Jayswal, *Manu & Yajñ yavalkya*; p. XXIII.

114. *Mānava Dharmaśāstra*; II, 242.

115. *Ibid;* IX, 253. The emphasis is shifted from are aryans to live as aryans suggesting fusion of races and the Brāhmaṇa revival stress the point. In Magadha there must have been such a fusion.

116. *Ibid*; IX, 260.

117. Shamasastry, *Arthaśāstra;* p. 45.

Chapter V

Condition of Buddhism in the Period between the Fall of the Mauryas and the Rise of the Kanishka group of Kushana Kings (188 B.C.—A.D. 78)

The period under study is equally noted for transition in the history of Buddhism. The Sanskrit—Buddhist literature exhibits this new trend. The convening of the fourth Buddhist Council in the time of Kaniṣka and under his patronage was an important landmark in the history of Buddhism.

This period is equally important for the reason that the great empire of the Mauryas was shattered. Aśoka in his life time endeavoured much for the development of Buddhism and he himself took pains of announcing Buddhism as the state religion. Needless to say that Aśoka was a great ruler and the patron of Buddhism as well. But after Aśoka the spread and further development of Buddhism became susceptible. For this it should not be misconstrued that Buddhism flourished only because of the state patronage. Besides Buddhism had some basic qualities that appealed to the masses.

In spite of all these, the protection and patronage of the state was invincible because other reactionary forces i.e. Brāhmaṇism had not died upto this period. It was necessary to safeguard this religion against those forces. It is also to be noted that when the state itself lost its potency with the passage of time, fortune of the further development of Buddhism was also questioned.

The last Mauryan emperor Bṛhadratha was murdered by a Brāhmiṇ—Puśyamitra sunga[1] Naturally when Puśyamitra ascended the throne, he took further steps to check the spread of Buddhism. The rise and spread of Buddhism did put a question mark on the fortune of Brāhmaṇism. The Buddha always condemned violence which was the basis of Brāhmanism. Aśoka and later Maurya emperors patronised Buddhism, so Brāhmaṇas were against the ruler too.

The condition of Buddhism in the present study is also important for the reason that this period witnessed frequent foreign invasions. The data available from inscriptions, coins, literature and art suggest that Brāhmaṇism was a living force in that period.[2] The performance of Vedic sacrifices was common. The Brāhmiṇs received handsome fees, in cash and kind from those foreigners who had accepted Buddhism.[3] According to Kern,[4] in the three centuries between the death of Aśoka and the reign of Kaniṣka, Buddhism was steadily on the increase in the North flourishing in the domains of the Bactrian Kings.

Puśyamitra, the founder of the Śuṅga dynasty, which succeeded the Mauryas in Magadha, revived Brāhmaṇism. In the *Divyāvadāna*,[5] he is described as one who wanted to surpass Aśoka by undoing the work done by him. He had the '*stupas*' and '*Viharas*' built by Aśoka razed to the ground. He put the price of 100 dinaras for the head of a Buddhist monk. This account of Puśyamitra's vendetta against the Buddhists seems to be exaggerated because a similar vengeance against the

Ajivikas and Nirganthas is attributed to Aśoka in the same text.[6]

In the period between the down fall of the Mauryas and the rise of the Kaniṣka group of Kuṣāṇa kings, we notice that Buddhism as a movement had split into many forces.These include the schools of *Sarvāstivādins, Mahasaṁghikas, Sthaviravāda* and *Yogācāra* etc. These different branches of Buddhism were the result of divergence of opinions and interpretations as to the tenets of Buddhism. Each school thought that its interpretation was original and sought to undermine the other school. Ultimate result was conflict among various warring schools, which could be checked by a strong man alone. This was really a phase of transition, marked by decadence. It was so partially because the Śuṅga kings were zealous propagators of Brāhmaṇism. It is however, not to suggest that the propagation of Brāhmaṇism was at the cost of Buddhism but the absence of royal patronage was no doubt a set back to the cause of Buddhism, which could have been kept united by a sympathetic king.

In the first century A.D. the Kuṣāṇas entered into India. The most noted ruler of this dynasty was emperor Kaniṣka. He rendered signal services to the cause of Buddhism but they were confined mostly to Gāndhāra and central Asia. It is said that he defeated the king of Pāṭaliputra but he left the city on the king's agreeing to part with Aśvaghoṣa, the famous Buddhist poet and dialectician and the alms-bowl of the Buddha. He made Aśvaghoṣa his spiritual instructor. He was perplexed by the different sectarian interpretation of *Buddhavacana* At his instance, a convention of the monks of all sects was held in Gāndhāra or Kashmir with a view to ascertain the correct meaning of Buddha's words. Aśvaghoṣa was the vice-president of the convention. The deliberation of the convention decided in favour of the views of Sarvāstivādins. While residing at Pāṭaliputra, Aśvaghoṣa had established his reputation as a great dialectician by defeating a very distinguished Brāhmaṇa teacher, and thereby securing the patronage of the then king of Mgadha.[7] It seems that about this time, the Brāhmaṇas of Magadha were very learned and proficient in dialectics and the Buddhist monks were no match for them. They won also the support of the ruler. Learning about the discomfiture of the monks of Vaiśālī at the hands of the Brāhmaṇas, Nāgārjuna, the renowned dialectician of the south deputed his disciple Āryadeva after giving him a thorough training in dialectics to Vaiśālī. With some difficulty Āryadeva persuaded the king to call an assembly of learned men to contest with him in controversies. The king complied with his request. Āryadeva defeated the learned Brāhmaṇas in arguments and convinced the king of his great erudition.[8] From that time the monks regained their position. Another monk, who came to Magadha after Āryadeva, was Gunamati, who was also very proficient in dialectics and was able to defeat his opponents.[9]

About the 1st century B.C. Buddhism underwent a distinct change towards Mahāyānism. The conceptions of Maitreya, the future Buddha, and of Amitābha, the eternal Buddha, were engrafted on the existing form of the religion, converting it gradually to a devotional one. Mahāyānism owes its origin to the Mahāsaṁghikas, who deified the Buddha and made many consequential changes as shown above.

The Mahāyānists incorporated most of the views of the Mahāsaṁghikas in their teachings and developed them further. The Mahāyānists accept the disciplinary rules of the Hīnayānists but with emphasis on dedication of one's own self to the service of others. Extreme altruism was the keynote of Mahāyānism and so the strict observance of the disciplinary rules was not insisted upon its followers. The Mahāyānists attached more importance to the fulfilment of the six perfections (parmita)[10] than to the observance of the monastic rules.

The fundamental difference between Hīnayāna and Mahāyāna was that the former sought emancipation through the realisation of the absence of individuality in the five constituents. The whole life of the Buddha from his birth to demise as also his pervious existences as depicted in the *Jātakas* and *Avadānas* was taken as the ideal by the followers of Mahāyānism, who regarded themselves as Bodhisattvas after the initial ceremony of taking the *Bodhicitta*, i.e. the vow that they would dedicated their lives in all of their present and future existences to the service of others.[11] From a study of the foregoing paragraph it appears certain that in the period between the fall of the Mauryas and rise of the Kuṣāṇas, like other parts, in Bihar also Buddhism had received a setback. The movement was fragmented and its propagation could not be carried beyond the limits of Aśoka's efforts.

Under the patronage of the great Mauryas Buddhism flourished at its high water mark. Also to say that those rules patronised and protected this newly founded religion to the extent far from their areas. But for a long time Buddhism could not develop as such in this territory.[12] It is not to say that the emperors remained passive during this period and maintained isolation from the development of Buddhism. The efforts made by the king, scholars, and the people of Bihar is not less significant.[13] The role of Bihar is recorded in the pages of the history of Buddhism, and it remains for today. Some Buddhist historians have described the Śuṅgas as the opponent of Buddhism.

It is also said that the king Puśyamitra did many harms to Buddhism. It is much controversial on which the historians should discuss.

There is no dispute over the fact that the destroyer of the Maurya empire, Puśyamitra was one of the champions of Brāhmaṇism and he revived Sanskrit.[14] Sanskrit reached at its zenith under the Śuṅgas. At that time, the philosophy, grammar, epic, history and the Purāṇas also developed to a considerable extent. Grammarian like Patanjali was the priest of the Aśvamedha

Yajña performed by the king Puśyamitra.[15] The '*Manusmrti*' which was considered as an ethic, appeared in revised edition at the same time. Most of the Purāṇas were written and compiled during these days. The great poet Kālidasa is taken to be a poet of Gupta period, but in real sense he was the contemporary of the Śuṅga king *Bhagvat* whose second capital was Ujjaini. Kāiidasa was the successor of Aśvaghoṣa.

According to Tibetan historian 'Tāranāth' Puśyamitra was the destroyer of Buddhism. On the basis of the stories of the '*Divyāvadāna*' Tạranāth says that the king Puśyamitra declared awards for the murder of a Buddhist monk when he reached Sialkot after the defeat of Menander. This way he tirelessly endeavoured to uproot Buddhism from the land through torturing and killing the monks. Buddhist historians maintained that he murdered many monks in the areas of the north India. But it appears that Tārānath and other Buddhist chronicles have written so due to their religious prejudices. The main point was that primarily Puśymitra was the supporter of Brāhmaṇism and secondly the destroyer of Buddhist like Brāhdratha and Menander. Menander wanted to over power the Magadha empire. He could have acted as a wise politician to kill Puśyamitra when he would have reached the capital city of Menander. There is much emphasis on it in the '*Divyāvadāna* so Puśyamitra is being described as the destroyer of Buddhism. In the Eastern part of India there was chaos and turbulence due to recurrent Greek invasions in Puśyamitra's time and before.[16] Demetrius invaded the empire in the period of Brhdratha and his son-in-law in the time of Puśyamitra. Puśyamitra killed Menander in 152 B.C. fighting in the valley of the Ganges.[17] He arranged an Aśvamedha yajña on the captive of the territories of Sindhu valley. Puśyamitra had deputed his younger son Vasumitra for the protection of the royal, who defeated the Greek army on the bank of the Sindhu.[18] Puśyamitra sent a letter at Vidisa to inform his son Agnmitra about the matter.

A question arises that if Puśyamitra used to give huge wealth for the murder of the Buddhist monks, then he would have also declared awards for the murder of the great monk like Nāgsena.

According to 'Milindapanha' Nāgsena was born in the area of Santhal Paragana in Bihar.[19] Sonuttar was his father.[20] Besides this, Nāgsena received his education in the 'Aśokarama Vihar' in Pāṭaliputra the famous capital of Puśyamitra.[21] Puśyamitra was commander-in chief there. The fact is that the guru of Nāgsena was 'Dharmarakshita'. He was the principal of the institution 'Aśokarama Vihar'. It was a centre of the Buddhist learning. A businessman carried Puśyamitra to 'Aśokarma Vihar' even after knowing him a Buddhist monk. Nāgsena came to 'Aśokarma Vihar' to study the philosophy of Buddhism. If Puśyamitra was an opponent of Buddhism then it was quite impossible to patronise and protect a great institution like 'Asokarma Vihar' in his city. It is also mentioned that there were some Buddhist monks who preached freely. Among them Songupta, Aśvagupta and Mahaupasika were the chief Buddhist propagators. These names are mentioned in 'Milinda Panha'. Then a question arises as to why the cruel Puśyamitra left them untouched and unharmed. 'Milinda Panha' describes Menander as a religious bigot. 'Milinda Panha' also maintains that Menander did involve the contemporary emigrant Brāhmaṇas and saints in theological discussions and in case not satisfied with these arguments did often penalise them.[22] The book informs us that 'Sākala' remained vacant for twelve years because Menander rusticated all the religious preachers. It is true that Menander became a Buddhist. Brāhmaṇas were not permitted to go to 'Sakal' so it remained reserved for the Buddhist monks and preachers. There is no emphasis in 'Divyāvadāna' on Menander's negative characters because he was a Buddhist king but the characters of Puśyamitra has time and again been questioned.

Under the Śuṅgas, efforts made for promotion of Buddhism and for its existence is second to none. After Pāṭaliputra, Śuṅga's second Capital was at Vidiśā.

Sānchī stūpa near Vidisa was established during that period. Most of the scenes of Sānchi stūpa have been prepared on the basis of the stories of the Jātakas. The stories of the Jātaka were given a good position by the Śuṅga kings. Not only sympathetic but in the establishment of Sānchī stupa they helped economically. If all the Śuṅga kings were the opponent of Buddhism then it would be quite impossible to establish great building like these. "Bhārhut" was established at the same time. Both the stūpas represent the features of the architecture of Śuṅga age.

Some small stone temples were made in Bodh-Gaya which were the creation of the latter age. The art of the building of Bodh-Gaya has been taken from the Sānchi and Bhārhut. It was established by the wife of Śuṅga minister named 'Indragnimha' The mother women was 'Nagdeva' who took serious part in making buildings. She was the wife of 'Brahmamitra' a great minister of Śuṅga court. On the basis of some inscriptions we may say that 'Aryakurangi' had made a vihāra in Bodh-Gaya near the temple. The Chinese pilgrim Fa-hien had also visited that place. The vihāras made by the *mines* of the Śuṅga king prove that they had great sympathy for Buddhism.

The railings of Bodh-Gaya are no doubt the creation of the Śuṅga age. Besides the stories of the Jātakas, sun god is also painted on the railing. It shows the feeling of religious intolerance of the king. It still remains in the Eastern North direction of the temple. These evidences present the religious and cultural assimilation. The excavations of Kumharāra at Pāṭaliputra shows that they were different from the vihāras of Kuṣāṇa's period.[23]

The centres of art in the Śuṅga age were Śrāvasti, Kośāmbī, Bodh-Gayā, Mathurā, Sānchī, Pāṭaliputra and Bhārhut.[24] Many archaeological evidences are found in the museums.

In the Śuṅga age too, though it is called unfavourable for Buddhism, many steps were taken for its developement.[25]

Some Buddhist scholars like Nāgsena were born those days. The rapid growth of Buddhist teachings reached at its high water mark. The idols of Buddha at several places were established. Although it has been sought to be expounded that Śuṅga rulers were persecutors of Buddhism and that they were against Buddhism, yet there is no definite evidence either archaeological or of secular nature to suggest that either Puśyamitra or any of his successor did really involve in destruction of the Buddhist buildings. Rather to the contrary he undertook the construction of many buildings Buddhist in character

REFERENCE

1. B.N. Puri, *India under the Kushanas;* p. *140*
2. *Ibid;* p. 140.
3. *Ibid;*
4. Kern, *Manual of Buddhism;* p. 48.
5. A.L. Thakur, *Comprehensive History of Bihar* (ed); Vol. 1, Part 1, p. 845.
6. A.L.. Thakur, *op. cit;* p. 845.
7. Beal, *Buddhist records of the western world;* II p. 100.
8. A.L. Thakur, *op. cit.*; p. 846-47.
9. *Ibid;* p. 847.
10. The Six paramitas are *-dāna, śīla, Kshanti, vīrya, dhyāna and* prajñā See, A.L. Thakur, *op. cit.*; p. 849.
11. *Ibid* ; p. 850.

12. H. Tripathi, *Baudhdharm aur Bihar* (Hn); p. 184.
13. *Ibid; p.* 184.
14. *Ibid* ; p. 185.
15. B. Upadhyaya, *Prachin Bharat ka Itihas* (Hn).; p. 181.
16. H. Tripathi, *op. cit.*; p. 185.
17. Tarn, *The Greeks in Bactria and India; p.* 228.
18. *Ibid; p.* 229.
19. *Milinda Panha*, p. 1, 1, 6, 7.

    Tripathi, *op. cit;* p. 186.
20. *Ibid.*
21. *Ibid.*
22. H. Tripathi,*op. cit;* p. 187.
23. *Ibid* ; p. 188.
24. *Ibid.*
25. *Ibid;* p. 188.

Chapter VI

Transformation of Buddhism from the Time of Kanishka to the End of the Third Century A.D.

The Buddha appeared in the history of India in the sixth century before the birth of Christ with a new vigour and spirit to lead the religious thoughts of the age, aiming, at the liberation of mankind from all kinds of sorrow and sufferings. The sixth century B.C. was remarkable for advent of similar religious leaders in China, Greece, Iran and India. In the same period we notice the advent of religious leaders and masters of philosophy like Lao-tse and Confucius in China. Parmenides and Empedocles in Greece, Zarathustra in Iran and Mahāvīra in India.[1] But none of these teachers except the Buddha could influence people with their tenets so widely and deeply within and outside the boundary of their own countries where they had been born. The influence of the Buddha had been beyond measure both in the country of his birth India, as well as in other parts of the globe.

Buddhism directly concerns with the problems of human life and its logical and scientific solution.[2] The philosophy of

Buddhism was well demonstrated by Gautama, the Buddha in his own life. His own experiments were the conclusion of his doctrine. Buddha's search for truth, his means of attainment, and his method of preaching were based on his rational approach and practical experience. He began his spiritual career with a personal query from within as to the meaning of life whch apparently seems to be full of misery and suffering. He left home and hearth the abode of fullest wordly pleasure to realise the truth by which he could solve the problems of his life ever. After his self-realisation he called his method of spiritual experiments as "Ehi passika—come, have the experiment thyself, and get the result." This was exactly the method of Indian way of spiritual experiment.

The essence of all religion is a change in man's nature. Destruction of desire for sense enjoyment and manifestation of inner divinity is the central teaching of both the Brāhmaṇical and the Buddhist religions.[3] Unfortunately, at this time, the Brāhmaṇic religion lost this ideal. In this confused state of religious practices and hazy philosophy of both the Brāhmiṇs and the contemporary Śramaṇas, the *Śākyamuni* Buddha appeared with a demonstration of the perfection of spiritual attainments through his *Dharma* which was quite logical and easy to be followed by all.

The essential tenets of Buddhism had been explained by the Buddha in his first sermon at Sārnāth. It consisted mainly of the Middle path, Four Noble Truths and Eight-fold path to purify the mind for attainment of *nirvāna*. Regarding the Middle path[4] the Buddha's sermon was like this:

These two extremes, O monks, are not to be pursued by a person who has renounced the world for attaining the truth, which two? On the one hand that which is linked with the thoughts of sensuous pleasures (*Kāmesu*) which is low (hine) ignorant, Vulgar, ignoble (*anarya*) and profitless; and on the other hand which is connected with self-mortification and therefore is painful, ignoble and profitless." The Buddha suggested a middle course between too much austerity. His middle path was a new contribution to the traditional spiritual exercises which highly esteemed austerity and penance. Regarding the truth of pain and its cessation the Buddha said. "Now this, O monks, is the noble truth of pain; birth is painful, old age is painful, sickness is painful, death is painful, contact with unpleasant things is painful, separation from pleasant things is painful, and not getting what one wishes is also painful.[5] In short, the five khandas of grasping are painful "Now this, O monks, is the noble truth of the course of pain, that craving, which leads to rebirth, combined with pleasure and finding pleasure here and there, namely, the craving for passion. The craving for existence and craving for non-existence."

"Now this, O monks, is the noble truth of the cessation of pain. The cessation without a reminder of that craving, abandonment, forsaking release non-attachment."[6]

"Now this, O monks, is the noble truth of the way" that leads to the cessation of pain. This is the noble Eight-fold Path, namely, right view, right intention, right speech, right action, right livelihood, right efforts, right mindfulness and right concentration."[7]

The fundamental principle of Buddhism is the law of causation or Dependent Origination. According to this theory, the continuous existence of a being is like a wheel of causes and effects. Ignorance is the primary cause of all actions, from actions arise consciousness, forms (nāmarup), the six senses; contact, feeling, craving, grasping, becoming, birth and suffering. If we are to stop suffering, the effect, we must stop the primary cause, ignorance.[8]

The Buddha accepted the ancient Indian theory of Karma as it was accepted by many other wandering sects of mendicants of his time. The doctrine of Karma brings to responsibility of an individual that the deeds only done by him determine the state of his life. His deeds only determine whether he will be born or whether he will be free from the chain of births. It is Karma that differentiates alll beings from one another. Karma is not a pre-destined imposition on beings by any external power or agents like gods. The pre-Buddhist doctrine of Karma was elaborately developed and practised in life by the Buddha and his followers. The Buddha with all emphasis declared that a being has the freedom of will to act, to remove the evil effects of his previous births. Freedom from all Karma is the state of Nirvāna the total extinction of personality. As a lamp cannot produce flame if there is no oil, so a being cannot be re-born if he has no seed of Karma (action). Nirvāṇa is the extinction of the spring of action.[9]

The Buddha's analysis of the cause of suffering was logical and it was also in conformity with the prevailing theory of re-birth found in the Upaiṣads and doctrines of some other post-Vedic wandering monastic sects. The way shown by the Buddha to overcome the sorrow or otherwise to attain the blissful state of Nirvāṇa was somewhat novel, which could be practised by all. Buddhist methods distinctly differed from those of the Vedas and other contemporary practices of spiritual attainments preached by the non-Vedic mendicants.

To purify the mind, to make it free from desire and attachment— one should practise physical and mental restraint. The eight-fold practices like right action, right thinking, right livelihood, right contemplation, etc., are the common virtues to be cultivated. The Śilas or the codes of conducts for both the lay house-holders and the monks were prescribed by the Buddha. But the codes of morality prescribed by the Buddha were almost common with those of the ancient Rishis and holy sages of India.

The Buddha's direct aim and Nirvāṇa—nothing shorter or smaller than that. It required constant spiritual exercise and contemplation. According to the Buddha, an aspirant should cultivate the four noble sentiments—'Brahmavihāras'—to reach the goal of Nirvāṇa. The four noble sentiments are[10]—Mettā (universal love), Karuṇa (compassion), Muditā (sympathetic joy), and Upekkhā (equanimity). Cultivation of love, sympathy and attitude of service to others is a special contribution of Buddhism towards social behaviour of human beings. These feelings are restricted not only to the mankind alone, but they cover all beings of past, present and future; whether of this world or of other worlds. *Nirvāṇa,* the final goal is difficult to arrive at, but cultivation of love and compassion to others is not so difficult. This noble Buddhist spirit is much wanted by the humanity in all ages. Buddhism has always been popular for this noble attitude. Buddhist morality is inseparable from the spiritual practice[11]—which leads to the state of Nirvāṇa. The elaborate rules of conduct for the monks as nuns were prescribed by the Buddha himself and were known as Vinaya. The Vinaya the code of religious discipline is the guide of a follower of the Buddha. The Buddha in his parting message advised his followers to stick to the code desciplіne, Vinaya, in his absence.

The Buddha was conscious about the mental status of his lay disciples, the house holders most of whom were merchants, craftsmen, cultivators, public servants and simple women of their families. They could not aspire for the Nirvāṇa in that very state and in that very life. Buddhist doctrine of Karma was liberal and logical enough to assure all with the hope of Nirvāṇa in the next or in subsequent life by virtue of their noble deeds.[12] The house-holders, in most cases, were aspirant of immediate mundane profits along with the lofty of ambition Nirvāṇa. So the Buddha prescribed certain meritorious deeds to be performed by the house-holders by which they could attain a better and happier life in heaven or in this very world. The house-holder's performances of meritorious acts consisted in charities to monks, Brāhmiṇs and the needy people, worship of elders and ancestors and observance of fast and listening to sermons four times every month. They took the five vows of not to kill, not to lie, not to commit adultery and not to use intoxicants. On the days of *'Uposatha'* more vows were accepted.

The Buddha disapproved of superstitious rites, ceremonies, severe austerity detrimental to the body and mind and sacrifices where animals were killed.

The original *Dharma* of the Buddha was a way of life, of being and becoming pure in thinking, speaking and acting.[13] It was not an elaborate system of rites, worships and prayers as we find in modern times in many Buddhist sects. The Buddha was the first rationalist of the world who asserted that an individual need not rely on any exterior agent for this salvation from ths miserable state of life, but he himself should be the creator of his future, which would lead him to the goal of *Nirvāṇa.*[14] In course of time, the Buddhist ideal of self reliance, belief in the doctrine of *Karma* and observance of Vinaya rules prescribed by the Buddha have been remarkably transformed.

The division and further transformation that took place in Buddhism was not a peculiarly strange phenomenon. Buddha himself had the idea of the ensuing period when his philosophy would be transformed and it would be divided into many schools. This view may be corroborated with the fact that Itsing, the Chinese Buddhist pilgrim, records a story connected with an early Indian King, Bimbisāra of Magadha who ruled almost three centuries prior to Aśoka Bimbisara saw in a dream a piece of cloth and a stick divided into eighteen fragments.[15] The Buddha who was a contemporary of the king, is said to have explained him that these eighteen fragments represented the eighteen schools into which his philosophy would be divided after his death and that well over a hundred years after his *Parinirvāṇa* a king called Aśoka would come to the throne and would rule over the whole of Jambudvipa,[16] and would unite the schools. Clearly this is a legend which became current in the Buddhist world some centuries after the death of Aśoka.

So long as the Buddha was alive, his sayings and the rules set by him were the guide to the spiritual life of his followers both the monks and the laity. His practical concern was to guide his disciples towards the goal of *Nirvāṇa* through the golden mean of the Middle Path and by practising Śila, Samādhi and Prajnā. Though most of his disciples would abide by his codes of discipline, there were a few who would not accept his authority in some matters concerning religious practice and administration of the Sangha. His cousin Devadatta is said to have opposed his authority and tried to create divisions in the Sangha by demanding stricter disciplines in the life of the Buddhist monks.[17] There were other monks, too, who wanted to live an easier life with better food, dress and comforts. There were incidents which proved that difference of opinion arose among the monks which could not be controlled by the Buddha.[18] In some cases, he had to withdraw his presence from among the rival monks, being unable to reconcile them to a logical agreement. While at Kośāmbi, the Buddha heard that a quarrel was going on among the *Vinayadharas* (Masters of Disciplines) and the *Dharmakathikas* (Preachers of Doctrine) on minor matters of discipline.[19] The Buddha, being unable to reconcile the conflicting monks and being disgusted by their defiance, retired to a forest called *Parileyyaka.*[20] He was living in the forest alone taking more of his attendants with him, when it is said, he was attended by an elephant and a monkey. However, the monks of Kośābmi came to realise their mistakes and being repentant asked pardon of the Buddha. There were monks like Upānanda, Channa and Sadvargiya (Pali-Chabbaggiya) who would take the earliest opportunity to violate the rules of the *Vinaya.* There were some monks who would not like any restrictions on the life of a monk.[21] A monk, Subhadra by name was opposed to the rules of discipline.[22] It is said that on hearing the death of the Buddha, the monk felt a sign of relief saying that he was form that time free from the restrictions of "do this, do not do that"—imposed by the Buddha. It was the fear of many ardent and sincere disciple monks of the Buddha that his teachings might be misinterpreted by the perverted followers for their personal likings.[23] Buddha placed too much reliance on his Dharma the attachment of his followers to his *Dharma* and *Vinaya* which he supposed would be of the implicit type for ever.[24] He instructed his disciples that after his death his teachings would be their teacher. This is recorded in "*Mahāparinibbāna* Suttānta"[25] and forms also the subject of a dialogue between Ānanda and Vassākāra Brāhmana, the minister of Magadha.[26] Vassākāra asks Ānanda, "Has any Bhikshu been specified (by Buddha) as would after Buddhas death become the refuge (leader) of men under whom everybody would seek shelter." Ānanda answers in the negative. This tendency of challenge and defiance towards the codes of discipline (Vinaya) became prominent immediately after passing away of the Buddha. A council of monks was held at Rājagriha, after the passing away of the Buddha under the presidency of Mahākāśyapa where the sayings of the Buddha were recited, heard and critically recorded to be preserved for the next generation. But even some direct disciples like Pūrna could not fully agree with recording which, according to their memory, was different from the words of note master, the Buddha. The points of difference in most cases were relating to the rules of Vinaya to be followed by the monks. In course of time, different schools and sects of Buddhism were formed on the grounds of slight difference or on different interpretations of the same words of the master: "Common interests arising from personal attachment to certain persons or group of persons, or created by various causes, such as associations, studies, geographical regions, as well as honest differences of opinion that gathered strength in the course of time, probably led to the formation of different sects of schools.[27] Thus the original teachings of the Buddha had undergone a transformation of noticeable character in course of two or three hundred years of passing away of the master who had apprehended this dissension of division before his physical disappearance from this world. There arose as many as eighteen distinct sects of Buddhism in course of three hundred years, differing on very minor Vinaya rules or in different interpretations of the words of the Buddha councils of monks would be held from time to time, when such difference of opinions would arise to come to a settlement as to the real meaning, import and application of the sayings of the master, specially in matters of rules of conduct for the monks, when there was a confirmed disagreement, a new school would be formed with a section of monks holding the same views. Thus the number of Buddhist schools multiplied as time passed on. In course of their discussions, they interpreted the terse expression of the 'Teacher' in different ways, and introduced additional materials in the interpretations passing them in the name of Buddha to give them stamp of authenticity. This happened in most of the Parishads scattered over the whole of northern India. There was none at that time in the whole of the Buddhist community who could dissolve the numberless divergences thus originated into one uniform whole and convert the threatening centrifugal forces then at work into centripetal, conducive to the well-being of the whole Sangha.[28]

In countries outside India Buddhism had under gone further transformation in the names of new schools to suit the local demand and environments. A particular school under the same name might differ in practising the rules of Vinaya either omitting or adding or altering some of them.

After disagreement there arose two sects in the Buddhist Sangha—the Theravāda (*Sthaviravāta)* and the *Mahāsanghika.*[29] The monks who deviated from the original Vinaya rules were called Mahāsanghikas while the orthodox monks were distinguished as the *Theravādins.*[30] In course of time, these two sects were further divided into sub-sects. Thus eleven such sub-sects arose out of the Theravāda, while seven issued from the *Mahāsanghika*. Later, there appeared other sub-sects, the difference being very negligible and the followers being very few. We have an idea of some of the sects and sub-sects which were mentioned in the Buddhist literature.[31].

Before going into the details of the nature and philosophical divergence of these sects, it is almost necessary to trace out the factors and forces responsible for the split-away in the original Buddhist canons. In this connection, elasticity or the rules of discipline should be discussed first because it also played a role though at the superficial level.

The rules of conduct which were in the course of being deigned were not codified at the time. The Śākyaputtiya Samanas like other contemporary religious orders possessed a set of rules known as the 'Patimokkha' for their guidance and the disciples as to recite those rules every fortnight in the presence of the congregation, the bhikkus residing in the forests not being excepted.[32]

According to Beal and Minayeff[33] the practice of preserving the secred lore in one's own vernacular contribute also to the formation of schools. At present evidences are not strong enough to put this conclusion on a solid basis and we are not in a position to point to any particular school as the result of the operation of this factor alone.

It is well known from Buddha's life that his attainment of Buddhahood led him to adopt 'middle path' which eschewed austerities as a means of attaining to religious goal. This is an inconsistency which can be explained in two ways, first by holding that the passages were interpolated in later times by those disciples who were in favour of such practices, and secondly by the position that Buddha changed his attitude later on in view of the strong tendency of the people who took to or believed in the efficacy of the austerities and who could not be satisfied with a religion barren of such practices. In either case, we have to admit that austerities crept into Buddhism in early times and the adoption of these by Buddhists led to the formation of schools.

THE STHAVIRAVĀDINS OR THE THERAVĀDINS

The Theravādins are the orthodox followers of the teachings of the Buddha,which are recorded in the Pāli *Tripiṭakas.* This school accepts Gautama, the Buddha, as a human being, having qualities of superior personality with common pleasure and pain. The Theravādins follow the simple teachings of the Buddha which may be summarised as 'to abstain from all kinds of evil, to accumulate all that is good and to purify the mind.[34]

They also practice *Śila, Samādhi* and *Prajnā. Śīla* or good conduct is the very basis of purification of the mind which is full of desires, the seeds of births. Mainly five *Śīlas* are prescribed for the house-holders and for the monks there are many rules of conduct.[35] *Samādhi* is meditation, to keep one's mind perfectly balanced so that it may be possible to grain a proper insight into the real nature of things. *Prajnā* is the supreme knowledge which leads a man to the realisation of truth. The Theravādins accept the doctrine of *Karma* and hold that the action of an individual is responsible for his bondage or liberation.

The Theravādins[36] consider that all worldly phenomena are subject to three characteristics, they are transcient (*anilya*), full of suffering (*dukha*) and non-substantial (*anātma*). The phenomenon or the exterior world is the creation of certain elements by our sense organs. The aim of a man should be the state of Nirvāṇa which free from passion. The state of *Nirvāṇa*, according to this school is beyond description. Buddha's silence as to the natrure of *Nirvaṇa* is thus explained by the Theravādins. This school follows the Middle path by means of Eight-fold noble actions believing on the doctrine of *Karma.* When an aspirant attains Nirvāṇa, he becomes an '*Arhat', a worthy man. Arhathood* is the final goal from where there is no more return to wordly life. The Theravādins are satisfied with their own Nirvāna, they do not bother for others.

THE MAHIŚĀSAKAS

There were two groups of this school. This school had its origin from *sthaviravāda.* But according to Vasumitra, this school was derived from the *sarvāstivāda.*[37] This school had its branch in Śri Lankā. Like the Theravādins, the earlier *Mahiśāsakas* believed in the simultaneous comprehension of truths. According to them past and future did not exist, only the present and nine Asamskrta *dharmas* did.

The *Mahiśāsakas* like the Theravādins, believed that *Arhats* were not subject to re-births[38] as they overcome their desires. No god could lead a holy life and no heretic attain miraculous powers. They gave more importance to the Saṅgha than the Buddha.Therefore according to them, charities given to the Saṅgha were more meritorious than those given to the Buddha only. They did not follow all of the Eight-fold Noble Paths, some concerning only physical actions and not mental transformation. The later Mahiśāsakas held some contrary views to those followed by the earlier members of this sect. Like the *Sarvāstivādins,* they believed in the past, the future and held that the *skandhas, āyatanas* and *dhātus* existed to give birth for the next existence.[39]

THE SARVĀSTIVĀDINS

The Sarvāstivāda school was a later outcome of Buddhism, next to the *sthaviravada.*[40] This school maintained the spirit of the original Buddhism till the rise of the Mahāyāna in India. Vasubandhu during his early monastic life was a great champion of this school before his conversion to the Māhayāna faith under the influence of his brother Asaṅga. This school flourished in the North-west provinces of India in the 1st century A.D. Kaniṣka was a patron of this school. A Buddhist council was held during his reign to revise the canons of Buddhism. This school was based on the theory that everything exists (*Sarvamasti).* The expression in Pali '*Sabbhamatthi*' occurs in the Saṁyutta nikāya and this statement might be the foundation of this school which believed in the words of the Buddha.[41] It meant the existence of elements of the past and the future in the present (*Trikālasat*). If upheld that the present had its root in the past and the consequences in the future. In the widest meaning Sarvāstivāda maintained that everything existed everywhere at all times and in every way.[42] In course of time, this school was further divided into seven sub-sects, namely, *Mūlasarvastivāda, Kāśyapiya, Mahiśāsaka, Dharmaguptikā, Vahuśrutiya, Tāmrasātiya and Vibhajjavāda.* Buddhism was propagated to central Asia and China through this school of Hinayāna.

THE SAUTRĀNTIKAS OR THE SANKRANTIVĀDINS

This school originated from the *Kāśyapiyas.* The *Sankrantivādins* believed in the transmigration of the substance from one life to another. It also believed that every man had in him the potentiality of becoming a Buddha as it was believed by the Mahāyānists. This school was supposed to be link between the Srāvakayāna and the Mahāyāna.

THE MAHĀSAṄGIKAS

This school was formed by the earliest seceders who rejected certain portions of the sayings of the Buddha accepted in the first council held at Pāṭaliputra.[43] They made a new compilation of the *Dhamma* and *Vinaya* in their own way with the inclusion of those rejected in Mahakassapa's council. The new compilation of the Mahākasaṅghikas was known as the *Acāryavāda* (sectarian teachings) while the original one was known as the Theravāda (orhodox doctrine). It is said that the Sainghikas has composed their canon in Prākrta. The texts of this school were translated into Tibetan and Chinese in the later centuries. The Chinese travellers and scholars referred to these texts widely.

The Mahāghisanikas accepted the fundamental teachings of the Buddha as the Theravādins did.[44] According to them, the Buddhas were free from all impurities. They had the supreme power of recollection of the merit of previous births. They were always absorbed in meditation, their birth was a divine process, they had no sleep or dream everything them was transcendental (lokottara). According to the Mahāsanghikas there was no existence of being after death and before birth.

The *Mahāvastu* or the *Mahāvastuavadāna* is the original work of the Mahāsanghika sect. In course of time, the Mahāsanghika sect was split up in other minor sects like *Ekavyāharika, Lokottar vāda, Kokkuṭika (Gokulika), Bahuśrutiya, Prajnaptivada* and the *Śaila* schools. The *Bahuśrutiyas* and the *Caityakas* were later off-shoots of the *Mahāsanghika* sect and differed in minor points from the original. The Mahāsanghikas differed from other sects in doctrinal matters, rules of discipline and colour and manner of robes of the monks. The ten points as given in the Pali and other texts are also stated by Yuan Chwang in his account of the Council at Vaiśāli. A remarkable difference between Yuan Chwang's account and the traditions in the Pali and other texts is noticeable in connection with the Mahāsanghikas at the meeting of the Council at Vaiśāli. According to the former, the Mahāsanghikas renounced all their deviations from the orthodox rules and took to those that were approved by the Theravādins.[45]

The principal objective of the Mahāsanghikas in seceding from the main body of orthodox Buddhists becomes apparent to us by a glance at the subject matter the rules regarding which they differed and the doctrines which they turned to profess.

A branch of the Mahāsanghikas, this school had its origin to a teacher who was very learned in the Buddhists lore. This sect held that the teachings of the Buddha regarding '*anitya*' (transitoriness), '*Dukḥa*' (suffering), '*Sunya*' (non-attributes), anātma' (non-soul) and '*nirvāṇa*' (the final bliss) were lokottara (transcendental) since they led to emancipation. His other teachings were *laukika* (mundane).[46]

The Bahuśrutiyas are sometimes described as a link between the original Theravāda and the later Mahāyāna school, as they followed the teaching of both the schools. According to Paramārtha this school reconciled the two principal systems of Buddhism —the *Śrāvakayāna* and the *Mahāyāna. Satya-Siddhi śāstra* is the principal text of this school.[47]

THE CAITYAKAS

Mahādeva was the teacher of this school which originated in the later years of the second century after the Parinirvāṇa of the Buddha.[48] The founder of this school used to live on the top of a mountain in a Caitya for which this sect was called Caityaka. Other reason for the name of this sect was that it would consider worship of the caityas as an act of merit for attainment of Nirvāṇa.[49] This sect was prominent in south India specially in the Andhra Pradesh.

In doctrine, the *Caityakas* were almost same with those of the *Mahāsaṅghikas.* The Caityakas emphasised the devotional aspect of worship of the relics of the Buddha which was rather discouraged by the Buddha in most of his discourses. This sect believed in heaven to enjoy fruits of meritorious acts after this life.[50] They believed that the Buddhas were not subject to any attachment, delusion and ill-feelings to others. According to them the state of *Nirvāṇa* was a positive blissful state. Devotion or bhakit towards the Buddha and his relics held by this sect might be regarded as a step towards growth of the Mahāyāna faith which is a further transformation of the original Theravāda Buddhism.[51]

PRAJNAPATIVĀDA

This sect had many things in common with both the Mahāsaṅghika and the Sarvāstivāda sects. Accoring to the view of this sect *Skandhas* and *dukḥas* were not concommitant. It held that twelve āyatanas were not real. It believed strongly in the doctrine of Karma.[52]

In course of time, most of these sects lost their identity and merged in other prominent sects. Four sects, namely, *Vaibhasika, Sautrāntika, Mādhyamika,* and *Yogācāra* became distinclty prominent in course of time. Originated in Inida, these sects had their acceptance in many countries outside India, specially in the countries which were the followers of Mahāyāna Buddhism. These schools were very often mentioned in non-Buddhists literature of after days.[53]

The *Vaibhāṣika* school found its origin on the Vibhāsā or commentary of the teachings of the Buddha leaving the Sutra text. The seven Abhidharma texts formed its general foundation. The Vaibhāsikas were believers in the reality of both mind and external objects. According to them *Nirvāṇa* was a perfect state of bliss.[54]

The Sautrāntikas recognised the validity of the Sutra or the original sayings of the Buddha. It flourished in fourteenth century after the *Mahāparinirvṇa* of the Buddha. Like the *Vaibhāṣikas* this school also admitted the reality of both the mental and external objects. It also held that all dharmas were void and unreal. Nirvāṇa, to them, was not a real object. Opposed to the Sarvāstivādins the Sautrāntikas were known as the Sarva-Vaināśikas—destroyer of all.[55]

The Mādhyamikas were so-called because they recognised the Middle Path (*Madhyamā Pratipad*) only as authoritative. The Buddha in his sermon at Sārnāth preached the doctrine of the middle path. It followed the middle course avoiding the two extremes of self-mortification and the life of extreme sense pleasures. The philosophical outlook of the Mādhyamikas was non-acceptance of the two views of existence and non-existence, eternity and non-eternity, self and non-self, etc. It advocated neither the theory of absolute reality, nor the theory of total unreality but only of reality. The ultimate reality, according to this school, was Śūnyavāda. It was also known as the Sūnyavāda. The Middle way pointed by the Buddha was different from the Middle view of the Śūnyavādins.[56] Nāgārjuna, the greatest philosopher of the age (2nd century A.D.) was the first teacher of this school. He wrote many treaties on this school which were translated in Chinese and Tibetan languages.[57] Āryadeva, Buddhapālita, Chandrakirti, Śāntideva and others were the later masters of the school. Two philosophic schools of Chinese Buddhism, namely, Tien-Tai and San-lun originated from the Mādhyamika sect of the Indian Buddhism.

The *Yogācāra* school was known as such as it emphasised on the practice of *Yoga*, the meditation. Meditation is the most effective method to attain the highest state of consciousness, the Nirvāṇa or the Buddha-hood. It was also known as the *Vijānavāda*, as it held Vijāna or the pure consciousness to be the ultimate reality. It taught subjective idealism, only thought reality, other things were unreal like dreams or mirage.

Ācārya Vasubandhu's view that *Citta* or *Vijāna* was the only reality, was the foundation of this school.[58] It was a changing stream of consciousness like flowing water. When Buddha hood would be realised, the flow would stop. According to some scholars Maitreyantha, the teacher of Asanga was the founder of the Yogācāra school.[59] Dignāga, Dharmapāla and Dharmakirti were some other great teachers of this school. All these schools lost their original characters and in course of time, they merged into one another to form two new patterns of Buddhism, broadly known as the Hinayāna and the *Mahāyāna*.[60]

TRANSFORMATION OF MAHĀYĀNA

Division of Buddhism into *Hinayāna* and Mahāyāna is rather superficial. Broadly speaking, those who follow the Theravāda doctrine based on the Pāli texts are known as the

Hīnayānists by the non-Buddhists and those who follow the tenets of later Buddhism are known as the Mahāyānist.[61] *Hīnayāna* is by no means a lower or inferior path and a Theravādin never calls himself a Hinayāni. Theravadins feel satisfied that they only follow the pure doctrine of the Buddha.

The Theravāda or *Hīnayāna* form of Buddhism prevails mainly in Ceylon, Burma, Thailand, Cambodia, Bangladesh and in some parts of India. The Mahayana form of Buddhism of prominent in Tibet, Nepal, China, Mongolia, Japan and some parts of India and middle Asian countries.[62]

The Mahāsanghikas, who separated themselves from the Theravadins were the pioneers of Mahāyāna movement. The Mahāyānists Cherish for Buddha hood and believe that the Buddhas are lokottara (supermundane). They also believe in the ten stages (Dasa-Bhūmi) of spiritual progress of a Bodhisattva for realisation of the truth.[63] The Mahāyāna form of Buddhism is based on nine great works of later origin—which were composed in Sanskrit. These are *Prajnaparamita, Saddharmapuṇḍarika, Lalitavistara, Lankāvatāra, Suvarṇaprabhāsa, Gandavyūha, Tathāgataguhyaka, Samādhirāja and Daśabhūmiśvara.*[64] These books are treated as holy as the sayings of the Buddha; it is interesting to note that in countries outside India, each of these texts formed a separate school of *Mahāyāna.* Some schools may honour more than one of these nine texts.

The ideal of the *Mahāyāna* is "Buddha hood for all." Mahāyāna assures that perfection can be attained by all. The ideal of the Hīnayānist is Arhatship which is attainable by a few through practices of discipline prescribed by *Śākyamuni* the Buddha.[65] Another difference between the two schools is very remarkable. A Hīnayānist is contented only with his own Nirvāṇa, while a Mahāyānist strives for Buddha-hood of other beings before his own.[66] The Mahāyāna aim is to serve others and to promote all beings to Buddha hood, even at the cost of self.

Conception of Bodhisattva ideal is a great landmark in transformation of Buddhism. Mahāyāna has its greatest appeal to the common mass only because of his ideal of sacrifice for the good of others for the happiness of others.[67] The original command of the Buddha to his disciples was to move about the world for the happiness of all beings—including gods—"*Vahujanahitāya, Vahujanasukhāya.*" Even in the modern world of selfish pursuits the ideal of the Buddhists plays an important part for generation of a feeling of universal brother-hood and peaceful co-existence.

Bodhisattva means—"*knowledge-perfect*"—one in whom there is essence of perfect wisdom. in Buddhism specially in the Mahāyāna, it means a "Buddha in the making"—one who is on the way to Buddha hood but not yet obtained it.[68] According to the Mahāyāna a Bodhisattva takes a vow that he will become a Buddha for the salvation of the world while an *Arhat* of *Hīnayāna* seeks only his own salvation, *Nirvāṇa.*[69] A Bodhisattva desires to undergo all the worldy miseries to make others free from its even at the sacrifice of the fruit of his own meritorious deeds. This noble ideal of service and self-sacrifice is recalled even at the modern crisis of selfish conflicts and aggressive violence.[70]

A Bodhisattva by practice of six pāramitās (noble deeds) will progress in the way of Buddhahood. The six practices are Dāna (gift), Śīla (morality), Kṣānti (forbearance), Vīrya (energy), Dhyāna (meditation) and Prajñā (wisdom). In the final stage the Bodhisattva will realise the Dharmaśūnyatā (non-existence of all things of the world). The fundamental principle of purification of the body and the mind by noble deeds (Śīlas) is accepted by both the Hīnayānists and the Mahāyānists.[71]

The noble ideal of four Brahmavihāras like Maitri (friendliness), Karuṇā (compassion), Muditā (kindliness) and Upekṣā (difference) is also respected by all for which Buddhism has a universal appeal. Judged form the ultimate motive, the aim of the Hīnayāna and the Mahāyāna is but one. *Nirvāṇa* or the perfection or Buddha hood is the goal, the noble truths of the Buddha are the ways, the base is the doctrine of *Karma.*[72] Mahāyāna is but a later development to suit the time and place.

FURTHER TRANSFORMATION OF MAHĀYĀNA: TANTRA

Theravāda, the original form of Buddhism had its direct aim to *Nirvāṇa,* as shown by the Buddha in his personal life through the practice of *Śīla* by which the mind would be free from all sorts of mundane desire. Mahāyāna also aimed at the same goal, Nirvāṇa, but not for one self only but for others too.[73] Conceptions of Bodhisattvas and many Buddhas along with spirit of service towards all beings brought a new dimension in the Buddhist thought and religious practices. The new spirit is Mahāyāna.[74]

Most of the house hold devotees and same of the monks were not prepared to run direct towards the goal of Nirvāṇa while their minds were hankering for sense pleasures either in this very life or in the life death. Mahāyāna assured all for the final bliss, at the same time it did not deny the fulfilment of mundane desires which were natural in majority of the aspirants due to Saṅskāra of previous births. So, the Mahāyānist of the later age added some scope and hope for mundane pleasure to the practice of spiritual goal, the Buddha hood.

By the eight and the nineth centuries A.D., Mahāyāna accepted some religious practices by application of *Mantras, Dhāranis, Mudrās, Maṇḍalas,* etc. which were unknown to the Theravādins.[75] These practices were supposed to bring merits for the mundane happiness as well as for spiritual achievements. These acts were known as Tantricism which were also followed by many non-Buddhists from time immemoral. The latest transformed Buddhism may be called *Tantric Mahāyāna Buddhism.* This type of transformed Buddhism with many rituals and worships of different gods and spirits is even now common with many Buddhist of the Northern countries.[76] The *Tantric*

Mahāyāna Buddhism also had many sects like the *Mantrayāna, Vajrayāna, Sahajayāna* and *Kālacakrayāna.* It is very difficult nowadays to point out the subtle distinction between these different Yānās. The aim of all Yānās is but one, attainment of the perfection, i.e. the Buddha hood, only the methods differ.

According to *Mantrayāna,* only applications of particular *Mantras* (incantations) are the principal means for attainment of salvation. This system of 'Japa' or repetition of an incantation is very common in almost all religions.

Vajrayāna is a form of *Mahāyāna* according to which '*Vajra*' is the principal means by which salvation is attained. *Vajra* in a special sense means *Śūnya* (void) or *Vijāna* (consciousness of ultimate truth). the state of enlightenment is the Vajra, when an aspirant attains the *Bodhi-citta,* he becomes as strong as the 'Vajra'—thunderbolt. He is known as *Vajradhara* or *Vajrasattva.* This system admits assistance of a guru or a spiritual guide.[77] According to Winternitz, "the *Vajrayāna* is a queer mixture of monistic philosophy, magic and erotics, with a small admixture of Buddhist ideas." (M. Winternitz, A History of India literature, Vol. II, page 388).

Sahajayāna is but a later form of Vajrayāna. The concept of the Bodhi-citta is different in this school. Bodhichitta is the united form of Śūnyatā and Karuṇā, Śūnyatā is conceived as *Prakrti* (female) and *Karuṇā* as *Puruṣa* (male). *Bodhi-citta* is like the union of a male and a female when an indescribable happiness arises. This type of happiness is conceived as the final experience of a *Sahaja* follower.[78]

Sahajayāna does not recognise the necessity of worship, mantras, mudrās and maṇḍals as it is done by other Mahāyāni Buddhists, Traits of *Sahajayāna* are noticed even today in many sects of non-Buddhist religions of North-east India and Bengal.[79]

Kālacakrayāna is an off-shoot of Vajrayāna, another aspect of meditational practice. *Kālacakra* means union of Śūnyatā and Karuṇā. *Kālacadra* is the root of origin of all creation, it is eternal. It is the ultimate reality and the Buddhas are born and reborn in it. Kāla (time) is changing from present to past and to future.[80] The main object of the Kālacakrayānist is to check the ever changing nature of Kāla and go above its influence. This school practices some kinds of meditation which helps control of five kinds air in our body.[81] This sect respects particular position of stars in the sky and counts the importance of *tithi*, *nakṣatra,* muhurta, etc., in meditational practices. Thus Astronomy and Astrology play an important role in this system.[82]

Tibetan Buddhism or *Lāmāism* is greatly influenced by *Kālacakrayāna* which is still a living practice in Tibet.

All the tantra Mahāyāna schools depend on the *gurus* (preceptors) for attainment of success in meditation and religious practices. The guru is respected as a god or as a Buddha, whose grace is highly valued for success in spiritual life. The Dadhanā of Mahāyāna Tantra is highly secret and transmitted only by the guru to his disciples. The teachings are recorded in obscure languages which can be explained only by the gurus.[83]

The transformed Buddhism in the form of different Yānās and the tantras gradually merged itself in to popular form of Hinduism having little or no difference at present.[84]

Theravāda Buddhism and transformed Buddhism with their different schools may be noticed to exist side by side in India.[85] But the great influence of Hinduism absorbed most of the Buddhist ideals and accepted the Buddha himself as an *Avatāra.* In India, the Hindus are happy and proud to accept Buddhism as one of the different branches of Hinduism. Buddha-worship and pilgrimage to the holy places associated with the memory of the Buddha are gladly accepted by the modern Hindus.[86]

Buddhism has revived the spirit of Hinduism to overcome the individual and collective misery with a belief in the doctrine of *Karma*. The Buddhist ideal of Śīla, the good conduct, is a universal need for social discipline, cultural growth and peaceful co-existence of human beings with an aim to reach a state of mind where all diversity is merged into oneness.[87] It is interesting to note that revival of Buddhism in the present age is aiming towards a new interpretation of the sayings and the philosophy of the Śākyamuni aiming at the greatest happiness of greatest number "*bahujanahitāya, bahujanasuphāya,*." The latest political thoughts and economic plans are to be based on the conception of human welfare of which Buddhist ideal is the way, the path. In most of the progressive countries of both East and West Buddhism is being studied and practised in the new perspective of "liberation for the self and welfare of the world." This neo-Buddhism is the latest transformation accepted by the modern age.

In conclusion it may be said that the *Sarvāstivādins* were like the Theravādins, a conservative school of the Hināyāna. They held almost the same views as the Theravadins believed in the non-existence of soul impermanence of material composites, the law of *Karma* and *Nirvāṇa* to be attained by transcendental knowledge.[88] Both the schools admitted the continual flux of elements or in other words the monetary existence of everyone looked upon the elements of the past as disappearing to give rise to the present and the present giving rise to the future. On account of their belief in the "*astitva*" theory of elements, they have analysed the material composites into various classes of elements which they enumerated in their philosophy.[89]

REFERENCE

1. The sixth century B.C. may almost be described as a period of universal questioning. Pythagorus, Confucius, Buddha &

Mahavira represent the same period. Romila Thapar, *Aśoka and Decline of the Mauryas,* pp. 4-6.

2. Nor were there religious and social trends isolated from certain economic changes of a fundamental nature. Aryan economy has changed from what it was during the Vedic period. Together with this the Buddhist period saw the opening up of extensive trade, and the increasing importance of that class of society associated with trade, the Vaisyas. Here again the material improvement of the Vaisyas through trade strengthened their antagonistic the feelings towards the unjustified privileges that Brahmanas and Kshatriyas had taken to themselves. R. Thapar, *op. cit.,* p. 5.
3. An article by Rahul Sankrityayan, *Buddhism: Marxist Approach.*
4. *Ibid.*
5. D.T. Suzuki, *Outlines of Mahāyāna Buddhism,* p. 140.
6. S. Dhar, *Transformation and Trend of Buddhism in the 20th Century,* p. 18.
7. *Ibid.,* p. 22.
8. *Ibid* ; p. 26.
9. N. Datta, *Early History of the Spread of Buddhism and the Buddhist Schools,* p. 110.
10. Buddha's Dhamma is thus detail by him; (i) Four Satipatthanas, (ii) Four Sammappadhanas, (iii) Four Iddhipadas, (iv) Five Indriyas, (v) Five Balas; (vi) Seven Bojjangas, (viii) Eightfold path. See Dīgh. Nik XVI, 50; Majjh, Nik; II. pp. 77, 103, 104.Lalita Bistara (Bibl. Ind.), a book of the Sarvastivadins, pp. 34-37
11. An article entitled "Buddhist Dialetics" by Rahul Sankrityayan in *Buddhism: The Marxist Approach,* p. 7.
12. S. Dhar, *op. cit.,* p. 19.
13. *Ibid* ; p. 32.
14. *Ibid.,* p. 33.
15. Takakusu edition (1986), pp. 13-14. Also see, Romila Thapar, *op. cit,* p. 26.

16. Jambudvipa, or 'The Island of the Rose Apple' was the name given to the southern continent of the earth in the orthodox Hindu cosmology. This region had human inhabitants, and the southern part of it was India.
17. S. Dhar, *op. cit.*, pp. 25-30.
18. *Ibid.*
19. *Ibid.*
20. *Ibid.*, p. 29
21. *Ibid* ; p. 29.
22. *Ibid.*, p. 89.
23. *Majjh. Nik*, II p. 105. According to the Samagam Sutta, Buddha hears of discussion in the India community as soon as the leader Nigantha Natputta was dead. He was afraid of like dissensions in his Church after his death but consoled himself that there was no difference of opinion among his followers in regard to the Dhamma preached by him.
24. Kinit Sutta in *Majjh. Nik;* II., p 103.
25. Pasadika Suttanta in *Digh. Nik.*, XXIX, p. 121.
26. Digh. Nik., XVI, 6,6,1. Also See, N. Dutta, *op. cit.*, p. 111.
27. Vapat, P.V. 1976, Principal school and sects of Buddhism. In self (ed.): *2500 years of Buddhism;* p. 87.
28. *Ang., Nik.*, I, XIV, I.
29. *Sam., Nik.*, II, p. 157.
30. *Ibid.*
31. *Majjh. Nik.*, III, P. 118.
32. *Ibid* ; 11, pp. 8, 9.
33. Minayeff's introduction to Pali Grammar; Beal's Abstract of four lectures on the Buddhist literature in China, p. 49. Also see, N. Dutt. *op. cit.*, p. 118.
34. *Dhammapada: Buddhavagga*, verse 5.
35. Oldenburg's Introduction to the *Vinaya Pitaka,* I, p. xiii.
36. Theravādins were otherwise known as the Vibhajjavadins, Dr. Oldenburg was uncertain as to the identity of the two names

and the classes they denote, but after *compassion* of the lists of schools, he found out that Vibhajjavada was but another name of Theravad. Oldenburg's Intro. to *Vinaya Pitaka*. I, p. xiii.

37. S. Ḍhar, *op. cit.*, p. 41.
38. *Ibid* ; p. 59.
39. *Ibid.*, pp. 62–63.
40. *Ibid.*; p. 66.
41. *Ibid* ; pp. 102-103.
42. *Ibid.*, p. 106.
43. It was about a century after Buddha's death that we meet with the great division in the Buddhist Church, a division between the conservative and the liberal, the heirarchic and democratic. Rhys David's *Points of* Controversy; p. xix.
44. The ten points, which the Theravādins considered as breaches of the rules of discipline, caused the conflict between them and the Mahasanghikas; N. Dutt., *op. cit.*, p. 125.
45. Watter's, *Yuan Chwang*; II, pp. 75-77.
46. Rockhill, *Life of the Buddha,* p. 180.
47. *Ibid.*, p. 184.
48. A few of these messages in Buddhist Sanskrit are deposited in the library of the Asiatic Society of Bengal.
49. *J.R.A.S.*, 1891.
50. N. Dutt. *op. cit.*, p. 159.
51. *Ibid.*, p. 160.
52. Rhys. Davids, *Points of the Controversy,* p. xix.
53. *Ibid.*
54. *Ibid.*
55. N. Dutt, *op. cit.*, p. 149.
56. V.A. Smith, *Early History of India*, pp. 267-268.
57. *Ibid.*, p. 270.
58. Yama Kami Sogen, *Systems of Buddhistic Thought*, p. 165.
59. *Ibid.*, p. 178.

60. *Ibid.*
61. For the tenets of the four schools, see Mahamahopadhyaya Dr. Satish Chandra *Vidyabhushana's Medieval Logic,* Ist edn., p. 66.
62. Takakusu, *I-tsing*, pp. 7-8.
63. Rahul Sankrityayana, *Buddhism: The Marxist Approach,* pp. 63-66.
64. *Ibid.*
65. N. Dutta, *op.cit.*, p. 88.
66. *Ibid.*, p. 102.
67. Rahul Sankrityayana, *op. cit.*, p. 39.
68. S. Dhar, *op. cit.*, p. 89.
69. *Ibid.*
70. Ibid., p. 128.
71. Translated from Chinese by Prof. J. Masuda in the C.U. Journal of Letters, I, p. 2.
72. *Ibid.*
73. G.D. De, *Democracy in Early Buddhist Samgha;* Preface, p. xi.
74. Eliot, *Hinduism and Buddhism*; Vol. I, p. 237.
75. Satkari Mukherjee, *The Cultural Heritage of India;* Vol. I, (2nd edn.), p. 587.
76. *Ibid.*, pp. 592-96.
77. J. Przyluski in "*Journal of Buddhist India*" (1927), pp. 36-38.
78. G.C. Pande, *Studies in the Origins of Buddhism,* p. 492.
79. *Ibid.*, p. 467.
80. N. Dutta, *op. cit.*, p. 132.
81. *Ibid.*, p. 84.
82. *Ibid.*
83. S. Dhar, *op. cit.*, p. 89.
84. *Ibid.*
85. P.V. Vapat, *op. cit.*, p. 96.

86. S. Radhakrishnan, *Indian Philosophy*, 2 Vols., p. 88.
87. *Ibid.*, p. 165, 92.
88. Yamakami Sogen's, *op. cit.*, p. 165.
89. Sogan, *op. cit.*, p. 119 and Kimura, *Original and Developed Doctrines*, p. 12.

Chapter – VII

Places of Eminence in the History of Indian Buddhism

The Buddha appeared in the history of India in the 6th century B.C. with a new vigour and spirit to lead the religious thoughts of the age aiming at the liberation of mankind from all kinds of sorrow and sufferings. The sixth century B.C. was remarkable for advent of similar religious leaders in China, Greece, Iran and India. In the same period we notice the advent of religious leaders and masters of philosophy like Lao-Tse and Con-fu-cius in China, Parmenides and Empedocles in Greece, Zarathrusta in Iran and Mahavira in India. But none of these teachers except the Buddha, could influence people with their tenets so widely and deeply within and outside the boundary of their own countries where they had been born. The influence of the Buddha had been beyond measure both in the country of his birth, India, as well as in other parts of the globe.

During the 6th century B.C. the whole of India was divided into sixteen Mahājanpadas and the dominance of Magadha was unquestioned. Buddha got his enlightenment on this land but his influence and the spread of his teachings may not be restricted to this land. Though this work deals exclusively with the rise and development of Buddhism in Bihar but in this chapter it is attempted to see Buddhism in its full bloom.

MAGADHA

It will be evident from what has been said in the previous chapters that Magadha was a suitable place for the origin and development of non-Brahmanic religions like Buddhism. If we look back to the remote period when it was known as *Kikaṭa*, it was even them considered by the orthodox Brahmanas as wanting in sanctity and unsuitable for the performance of sacrifices. It shows that it was for a long time disliked by the orthodox Brahmanas as a place of habitation and therefore, its inhabitants line in comparative freedom from Brahmanic orthodoxy. Hence we find in the *Majjhima Nikāya*[1] that Sakuhidayi Pari'›bajaka is telling the Buddha that in ancient times Magadha seethed with sophistic discussions. That this country was a centre of intellectual activity is evident from the *Samannaphala* account of King Ajatsattu's interview with six sophistic teachers.[2]

The *Brahmajālsutta* which was delivered by Buddha at Rājgṛha gives us a panoramic view of the various doctrines prevailing at the time. Many of the doctrines might be classed as Brāhmaṇic while the rest were non-Brahmanic.

Thus we see that the Buddha had to encounter the opposition of a large number of sects but fortunately he had to his advantage that there were several sects whose views were far from the Brāhmaṇic standpoint. There was however but a few rays of light in the gloom of opposition that darkened the path of progress and hindered him in his onward march.[3] He had phenomenal success in the Brahmanic villages of Khanumata and Ekanata where he could win over to his side two renowned Brahmanas kudanta and kasibharadvaja.[4] The piṭakas, though silent on Buddha's failure, mention as an example of Buddha's triumph over Mara, that in the Brahman village Pancasata, he could not obtain a single spoonful of rice in his begging round.[5] From this we get a glimpse into the volume of opposition that Buddha had to encounter on certain occasions. There are also in the Nikayas passing allusions to the firvolous grounds on which his opponents wanted to make his path thorny-some Brahmanas who wanted to rouse oppositions to him by saying that Buddha was wanting in reverence towards the aged Brahmanas and claimed superiority over them.[6] Buddha had also to meet opposition from the influential Brāhmaṇas, *e.g.* the minister of Ajatsattu who instigated other members of his caste to alienate the people from the Buddha by saying broadcast that all the blessings that man desired could be had from yajñas and they need not seek Buddha's help in the matter.[7] It was through his personality, his appealing way of preaching a rational *Dhamma,* his ability in deputations with the Brāhmaṇas and laying bare their weak points, and his firm stand against the abuses of belief and religion prevailing at the time that he could win over people including many Brāhmaṇas to his side.

Sanjay Belatthaputta, the centre of whose activities was at Rājgṛha, was the first non-Brāhmaṇic religious teacher to feel the power of the religion preached by the Buddha for within a very short time he saw that half of his following had been won over to the Buddha's side. .It was Assaji, a disciple of Buddha, who commenced the onslaught by converting Sariputta, the principal follower of Sanjay to Buddhism and Sariputta in his turn followed him until half of his quondam fellow disciples embraced Buddhism. This event together with the previous conversions made by the Buddha and his followers created in Magadha a sensation which served as the basis of the remark found in the Buddha took into his order 1000 Jatilas, 250 followers of Sanjay and the sons of distinguished Magadhana families.[8] Nigantha Nataputta was a formidable rival of Buddha, and as he was at work earlier than the Buddha, he made a fair progress in the spread of his religion in Magadha and the neighbouring states. It appears from the accounts of converts to Buddhism that Buddha could not convert the followers of Nataputta in large numbers, as he did the followers of other cults. But he stob a march upon Nataputta by being able to enlist among his upāsakas Bimbisāra and Ajātśattu who had been lay supporters of Nāṭaputta[9].

It has been so far dealt with the volume and nature of opposition met with by the Buddha in the different places in Magadha. It is now endeavoured to underline the Buddha's activities in Magadha in connection with the propagation of his religion as recorded in the Buddhist scriptures. The places which have been recorded as the scenes of his religious propaganda in Magadha are Gayā, Uruvelā. Rājgṛha and its suburb Nālandā, Pāṭaliputta, Dakhinagiri, Andhakavinda and Kallavalamuttagama.

Bodh Gaya is in the eye of a Buddhist the most sacred place on the earth, as it was the birth place of the religion which become almost pan-Asiatic in later times. Buddha's missionary work was started at Benaras, but it was when he visited Gaya after finishing his first activities at Benaras that we find the Buddha carrying on his missionary work at this place. Uruvelā, a village in the suburb of Gaya, was the stronghold of the *Jatilas*, an order of Brahmanical ascetics. They accompanied the Buddha to Gayạsisa where he delivered the discourse *Adittapariyayam* (Fire sermon) intended to explain to the Jatilas that the summum bonum which they wanted to attain through fire worship could be had not through the worship of fire but through the extinction of fires or 'raga' 'dose' and 'moha' kindled by the action of the sense organs on the objects of those senses. The Jatilas after hearing this discourse gave up their cults and joined the order initiated by Buddha as bhikkus.[10] It was with these bhikkus and the sixty one converts recruited at Benaras and its neighbourhood that the Buddha created a sensation at Rājgṛha.[11]

On the occasion of the Buddha's first visit to Rājgṛha in the second year after enlightenment, he stayed at *Latthivana*, five miles from the town. It was here that Bimbisara with his ministers, courtiers and village headmen came to meet him.

The importance of Rājgṛha from the point of view of missionary work was very great. It was a great resort of religious teachers and wonderers who used to come to the city usually in the company of the traders who supplied them with food and raiment in their journey from distant places. In the first few years after. Enlightenment, he spent his time frequently at these places with some of his distinguished disciples, viz., Sariputta, Moygatra, Mahakassupa, Arwnadha, Upali, Anand, and Devdatta delivering discourses and imparting them necessary training for their spiritual progress and missionary works.[12]

The Buddha utilized the opportunity of meeting the large number of emissaries sent to him in batches by his father Sudoddhana for taking him to Kapilvastu by converting them to Buddhism.[13] Sakutudayi, a playmate of the Buddha was the head of the last batch of the emissaries. After conversion he was able to persuade the Buddha to pay a visit to Kapilvastu.

While staying at Rājgṛha, the Buddha used to visit other places within Magadha with his bands of disciples. Only the places which rose into prominence by reason of establishment of monasteries and large number of adherents there have been recorded in the *Nikāyas.*

1. **Nalanda** : It was a small but a prosperous village situated at a distance of a yojana from gram Rājgṛha.[14] The usual residence of the monk was at the monastery Pavarikaambavana. There was another monastery midway between Rājgṛha and Nālandā called Ambalatthika where Rahula stayed at times.[15] From the nature of the discourse delivered there and from the particulars of the persons with whom the Buddha entered into disputations, it appears that Nigantha Nataputta had there a firm footing.[16]

2. **Pāṭaliputta** During the Buddha's life time, it was only a village called Pataligama which Buddha visited with his disciples in the last days of his life. The laity of place invited the Buddha and his disciples who on their arrival at the place were accommodated in a rest house probably known later on as the *kukkuṭa ārāma.* It was at this time that Sunidha and Vassakara, two ministers of Ajātasattu were fortifying Pāṭaligama as a defence against the vajjians. This fortified village afterwards rose to be *Pataliputta,* the capital of Magadha and great empire.[17]

Dakkhinagira : In the 11th year of Buddha's ministration, he visited the Brāhmaṇa village Ekanata and converted the two Brāhmaṇas Kasi-Bharadvaja[18] and Sompurna.[19] A distinguished female lay devotee velnkantaki Nandamata lived here.[20] It was at this place that the Buddha formed his idea of the way in which the *cīvaras* (robes of the bhikkhus) should be made out of pieces of cloth stitched together like the rectangular pieces of land tilled by different persons in the rice fields near the village.

Apart from these places, Andhakavinda and Kallavallamuttagama, two other villages near Rājgṛha, though not so well known had monasteries where the Buddha stayed at times. At Andhakavinda we find him instructing some newly ordained bhikkhus and converting Belattha Kaccana, a sugar merchant of the place. Mahakassapa while here at once to ford a stream to attend a Patimokkha assembly at Rajgṛha. After this incident the Vinay rule was instituted that a bhikkhu need not cross a stream, as wherever it exists, it should be made a boundary of the jurisdiction of a monastery, Kallavalamuttagama is important on account of its association with Moggalana who underwent there his first course of training.

KOŚĀLA

The kingdom of Kośala is next in importance to Magadha in the history of the spread of Buddhism. It was at Sāvatthi, the capital of Kośāla, that the Buddha spent almost the half of his career as a teacher[21] delivered the largest number of discourses and framed the largest number of Patimokkha rules[22], and it was here that the religion, which had passed its infancy in Magadha, developed into its full stature as found in the Nikåyas. Though according to Dr. Oldenberg[23], Kośāla was outside the limits within which orthodox brāhmaṇism prevailed, the territory was in fact within the said limits containing as mentioned in the Nikāyas, many Brahmana settlements. Dr. Oldenberg bases his opinion on two passages, one of the *cūllavagga* (XII. 2, 3) viz. "Buddhas are born in the puratthima janapads", and the other of the *Majjhima* Nikāya (II, p. 124) referring to Buddha as *Kośālaka*. The word *puratthima,* however does not imply prācyadeśa. The passage contemplates only Kapilvatthu lying on the northern extremity of Kośāla and not the whole of the territory and moreover both the town and the territory lay on the west of Sadānīrā, on early termit of Arayan colonization as mentioned in the *Satpatha Brāhmaṇa.*[24] Hence, as a citizen of Kapilvatthu, the Buddha could well be called a Kośalaka, though for the matter of that he was not an inhabitant of prācyadeśā. We, therefore, find that at the time of the rise of Buddhism, Kośāla was a Brāhmaṇical country, where the progress of the religion was not without its difficulties. The tracing of progress in the propagation of the faith in the kingdom is interesting in view of the above fact as well as for its inclusion of the home of the Śākya clan, to which the teacher had belonged.

Though Kośāla was Brāhmaṇical territory, it did not deter the Buddha from making attempts to spread his religion there from the very commencement of his carrer as a preacher. The first attempt was made at the time of his stay at Benaras through the first band of Buddhist missionaries, among whom figured the five inhabitants of Kapilvatthu and its precincts, namely the first five Brahmana converts of the teacher.[25] The second attempt was made by Buddha personally. While at Rājgṛha, he was repeatedly invited by Suddhodhaṅa and at last induced by Buddha's playmate Udayi to go to the place. During his short stay at the town on this occasion, he succeeded in converting some of the Śākyan youth of his time. The third and the most successful attempt was made at the time when he visited Śavatthi at the request of Anāthapinḍaka, who presented to the teacher the *Jetavana-arama* distinguished in later times as a great resort of bhikkus, and placed at his disposal all the influence that the could command for the propagation of Buddhism in Kośāla.

Inspite of the efforts of Anāthapinḍaka to give Buddhism a footing at Sāvatthi, the heads of the local sects resented the intrusion of a new religion into the field which they considered as their monopoly. The Buddha respected to meet a stubborn opposition from the leaders of the sects, and to ward it off, he had sent to Sāvatthi his ablest lieutenant Sāriputta entrusted with the ostimsible work of supervising the construction of the Jetavana Vihāra. Sariputta was a postmaster in the act of disputation and had deep knowledge of the Brahmanic love as well as that the non-Brahmanic sects. He had to enter into disputations with many teachers, all of whom he was able to silence by dint of his able exposition of the *Dhamma*.[26] A ground was thus prepared for the advent of the Buddhism at the time of the Buddha's arrival at the place. In addition to the opposition from the local teachers, the disciples of the six non-Brahmanic teachers were also at Savatthi to render thorny the path of the Buddha's in his mission. These people as also king Pasendi were great admirers of these teachers and used to speak of them as distinguished teachers of schools and heads of orders, and revered by the wise while of Buddha as young in age and fresh as a recluse.[27] Savatthi, according to the Uvasagadasao, was the head quarters of the Ajivika sect which held its founder Makkhali Gosala in very high respect.[28]

The opposition put forth by the six teachers and their disciples to the progress of the Buddha's mission was not so strong as that of the orthodox Brahmanas and Brahmanical teachers. They could not look with favour upon persons having no sympathy with their faiths and discouraging the observance of the forms and practices of their religion, not to speak of one who had raised the standard of revolt against same.[29] To some of the orthodox Brāhmaṇas, even the sight of the shaven-headed Buddha at the time of performance of sacrifice was considered ominous. The sight of Buddha at some distance was a cause for consternation to Aggika-Bharadvaja.

Evidences of hatred of Buddhism like those mentioned above can be multiplied but those that have been adduced are enough to show the antipathy felt by the Brahmanas of Kośala towards the Buddha and his disciples. The nature of the opposition encountered by the Buddha in the place accounts for many of the topics on which discourses were delivered by him or discussions were carried on with the local Brahmanas *e.g.* the origin of the caste system and the purpose it serves; inefficacy of sacrifices; absurdity of solving the indeterminable problems like the existence or non-existence of soul, permanence and impermanence of the world etc.; the falling of the Brāhmaṇas from the ancient Brāhmaṇic ideal, the truth underlying the belief in spiritual sanctification by battering in the rivers; the dependence of the Gods of the Brahmanic pantheon on the law of Karma, and so forth.[30]

The Brāhmanas of Kośāla had strong attachment to their religion and were lovers of truth. in which ever form it might be found. The Buddha achieved success in his mission in a great measure by appealing to this love of truth. He explained to them that the religion which they were following had in it a large measure of alloy which had diminished the value of the religion. The sites and ceremonies and false beliefs that grew round thc modicum of truth embedded in the religion served but to cover it with a thick coating of untruth. Buddha by his power of disputations and knowledge of the Brahmanic love brought home to the Brahmanas the truths that he was preaching. As soon as they saw the hollowness of their beliefs or the unsoundness of their philosophy, they with their characteristic love of truth embraced the religion which was placed before their eyes with all its charm. Some of them continued as laymen declaring their faith in the *Buddha, Dhamma* and *San'gria* while others went further and became bhikkhus. Rich and influential Brāhmāṇa householders like Janussoni,[31] Aggika-Bhardvaja,[32] and Dhananjani[33] professed themselves as lifelong upasakas of *Buddha, Dhamma,* and *Sangha.*

The distinct achievement of the Buddha in this Brahmanic country is the conversion of some of the distinguished Brāhmaṇa teachers who lived on grants of villages made by kings and were held in high respect by the people of the locality. In spite of their high positions as orthodox Brāhmaṇa teachers, and regardless of the advice and importunities of their disciples and admirers, the renowned mahasalas Pokkharasadi of Ukkattha[34], Lohicca of Salvatika,[35] and Canki of opasada took refuge in the Buddha and promised to be his followers upto the end of their lives. So great become Buddha's fame in Kośala that the sixteen disciples of *Bavari* came from as far a place as the bank of the Godavari to join the order.[36]

The greatest point of the Buddha's missionary career was spent at Jetavanarana in Sāvatthi. He resided here for twenty one vassas in addition to many of visits paid to it at other times. In this King Pasendi got many opportunities of meeting him and holding with him conversation on religious topics. From the references to Pasendi in the *Majjhima* and *ANGNTTA Nikāyas* and in the kosalasamytta of the s*aṁytta Nikayas,* it is evident that the king was a follower of the Brahmanic religion, had the Brāmaṇa Baveri as his first *purohita* and celebrated sacrifices involving slaughter of animals Victims,[37] one of his queens Mallika, and his two sisters Soma and Sakula, were lay devotees of Buddha.[38]

Though the infant religion could not at first secure patronage from the king, it did from Anathpinḍaka, a great magnate of Sāvatthi and the High Treasurer of the realm. His valuable advice combined with pecuniary help made it possible for the religion to strike its roots deep into the soil of Kośāla. It was he who organised the delivery of a few discourses by the Buddha to lay people regarding the duties of house holders and the place occupied by them under his religion. Thus it was Anāthpinḍaka through whose efforts a place was assigned by the Buddha to the lay Buddhists in the frame-work of his religion. The postponement of a due recognition of their relation to Buddhism, important as it was, would not have been conducive to the speedy development of the organisation, and through which the religion expanded itself.

The lay-devotee, who as a supporter of Buddhism ranked next to Anāthpinḍaka in importance, was Visakha, the daughter of a setthi of Sāketa, and wife of the son of a rich setthi of Savatthi. She persuaded her father-in-law Migara and other members of the family to give up their faith in the doctrines of Nigantha Nataputta and adopt those of Buddha. Her anxiety for the comforts of the monks and muns has become proverbial.[39] She built the Pubtsarama monastery where the Buddha resided for six vassas. It was at her instance that many of the Vinaya rules for both the bhikkhus and bhikkhunis were framed. Three other noteworthy lay converts of Kośala whose names may be mentioned in this connection are Gonaka Moggatana,[40] Pancakanga thapati and Isidatta-purana thapati who were all high state officials.

A notable incident connected with the Buddha's missionary work in Kośala is the radical change brought about in the life of Angulimala who was so turbulent that event the king of the realm could not restrain him. He turned a bhikkhu and ultimately reached *arahatship*. This conversion made a great impression upon the minds of the people of Kośala as also of the king,[41] and helped greatly the propagation of the religion.

Besides these territories, the Śākya territory will engage our attention here because the kingdom of the Śākyas falls within the limits of Kośala, the Śākyas were politically independent and formed a separate entity from the social standpoint with customs and practices peculiar to itself. They were followers of the Brahmanic religion and did not at first look with favour upon the idea of the Buddha launching a new religion in direct opposition to the time honoured ones. If we examine carefully the account of the reception accorded by the Śākyas to the Buddha at the time of his visit to the land of his birth after Enlightenment, it will be evident that there was a rift in the but welcoming his arrival.[42] The situation was so dismal that Buddha had to have recourse to miracles for bringing the Śākyas under control. Ultimately he made a few converts from among the Śākyas, some of whom came to be counted among the leading disciples of the Buddha.[43]

Nigantha Nataputta had been among the Śākyas sometime before the Buddha and secured some followers. Mahanama, a relation of Buddha, had Jaina leanings. To bring him round, Buddha delivered to him a discourse on the usefulness of the severe forms of self-mortification practised by the Jaina ascetics.[44] The result of this discourse upon Mahanama's mind has not been mentioned anywhere, discourses, but nowhere does he appear as giving up his faith to adopt Buddhism. He however appears as an interlocutor[45] in many discourses, but nowhere does he appear as giving up his faith to adopt Buddhism. The nature of the topics dealt with in the discourses delivered by the Buddha at Devadaha near Kapilavatthu suggests the inference that there were at the place a few followers of Nigantha Nataputta. There is no reference to the conversion of any of these Jainas to Buddhism. Moggatana who was with Buddha at the time succeeded however in converting vappa, a Śākyan Jaina to Buddhism.[46] The discourses delivered by the Buddha at Nigrodharma in Kapilavatthu speak of many lay devotees coming to hear them.[47] This as well as the fact that the Śākyans requested the Teacher to celebrate the inaugural ceremony of a new Santhāgāra at Kapilavatthu testify to the fact that by his preaching he succeeded in making his religion popular among the local Śākyas.[48] He could not however make any headway in the Brāhmaṇa village in the Śākyan territory, such as Silavati, Sakkara, Samagama, Catuma, Medlumpa[49] with the exception of the village khomadussa where all the Brāhmaṇas seated in an assembly embraced Buddhism after hearing the preaching of the teacher.[50]

This sketch of the spread of Buddhism in Kośala would not be complete without a reference to at least some of the various centres established within the territory for facilitating the propagation of the religion and the pursuit of spiritual exercises by the bhikkhus. The name of *Jetavana* rises first in our mind. As it is too well-known to need a description here, I pass on to the next important centre Pubbarama, a great monastery built by Vishākha six to seven miles to the north-east of the *Jetavana Vihāra.* It could accommodate a large number of monks and nuns in its numerous chambers while it afforded facilities for deep meditation in its secluded cells. On account of amenities of monk-life available here, it was a favourite resort of the Buddha and his disciples, the former passing there so many as six vassas.[51] The existence of the hermitages of Kalakarama, Kantakivana and Arjavana,[52] at sāketa is responsible for the name of the place as a resort of bhikkhus. It was very probably Visākha's father Dhananjaya, who was taking a leading part in the movement, made it Buddhist centre.

BUDDHISM AMONG LICCHAVIS

The territory to the east of Kośala and north of Årya and Magadha was occupied mainly by the various clans, namely the *Vajjis, Licchavis, Videhas, Mallas, Bhaggas* and *Koliyas.* All these clans lived side by side and most probably belonged to the same stock, and this accounted for the similarity of beliefs and practices that prevailed among them. Information about the ways in which the several clans except the *Licchavis* opposed the introduction of Buddhism, among them is extremely scanty. It is only about the *Licchavis* that we can give a running account. Though the territory of this clan lay outside the limits of the Brāhmaṇic middle country, yet Brāhmaṇism was here the prevailing religion. They however were not so orthodox as to prevent the non-Brāhmaṇical religions from taking root in their country.

Where the Buddha came among the Licchavis, Jainism has already run through a career of about 250 years from the time of Pāraśvanātha and had adherents in many of the *Licchavis.* This long career of Jainism in the kingdom of Vaiśālī was not there the only source of its strength. Nigantha Natputta, the reformer of Jainism belonged to a distinguished family of the Nala clan with wide influence in the land.[53]

Inspite of active opposition of this nature, the Buddha continued his work of conversion in right earnest. The high economiums showered on Buddha by the Licchavis at a meeting of their assembly, the freeling of wonder expressed by Mahanama at the sudden change of the Licchavis youths under Buddha's influence,[54] and the desire of Otthaddha Licchavi with a large retime to hear Buddha's discourses,[55] show that the Buddha could create a favourable impression on the minds of the local people and achieve some success in his missionary activities. As a mark of their devotion to the Buddha they dedicated to him not only the Mahavana Kutagarasala but also a large number of cetiyas which were also highly appreciated by him as places for meditation.[56]

One of the most important events in the history of Buddhism transpired at Veśālī. It was here that the Buddha gave his consent to the formation of the order of nuns at the importunities of Ananda and Mahapajapati Gotami. The latter had aheady advanced a little as a lay devotee in the path of sanctification at the time of conversion of Rahula and Nanda. It was after the death of Suddhodana that she in the fulness of her grief resolved to embrace the life of a recluse. She formed a band of recluses by bringing together a few ladies who had been bent on retirement from the world for some reason or other. With them she travelled under great physical stress and strain from Kapilavatthu to Veśālī where the Buddha was staying and obtained his consent to the formation of the order of nuns by agreeing to comply with the eight ordinances laid down at the time by the Buddha for the bhikkhunis.[58] She made a steady progress in spiritual culture under the guidance of Buddha and soon attained the highest stage of sanctification.

The Buddha passed through Veśālī in the course of his last tour. The only notable conversion made on this occasion was that of the famous courtezan Ambapalli who gave away her Arbavana to the Buddhist Sangha. It was while dwelling at capala cetiya situated on the outskirits of Veśāli that the Buddha resolved to end his mortal existence in three months.

The kingdom of Videha became in the pre-Buddhist days an important centre of Brāhmaṇic culture on account of king Janaka's enthusiasm and patronage of learning and spiritual culture which converted his court into an important meeting place of learned men especially from the western countries of Kośala and Kuru-Pañcāla.[59] The Makhadeva and Mahajanaka Jatakas and the Brahmayu Sutta of the *Majjhima Nikāya*.[60] testify to the prevalence of Brāhmaṇism in Videha at the time of the Buddha. The Nikāyas are silent as to the Buddha's missionary work in the place and the volume of opposition met by him there in the propagation of his religion. It is only in the *Majjima Nikāya* that we find that he stayed at *Makhadeva* ambavana of Mithila and converted on a certain occasion Brahmayu a distinguished and old Brāhmaṇa teacher.

Not so however fruitless was his work among the Bhaggas. The Buddha succeeded in converting three distinguished inhabitants of the Bhagga country, namely Nakulapita, Nakulamata, and Bodhirajakumara. There might have been other converts but their names do not appear in the Nikāyas The Buddha and his chief disciple Maggalana visited this place on two or three occasions and stayed at Sumsumaragiri Bhosakalvanamigadaya. The Buddha delivered a few discourses at the instance of Nakulapita and Nakulamata two of his most favourite lay disciples detailing the duties of house-holders.[61] The discourses delivered here by Meggatana relate to the means of overcoming passions.[62] It was while the Buddha was residing in this country that Bodhirajakumara requested Him to stay in his newly built palace Kokanda for a day sanctifying it by his presence, and give him opportunity of formally taking refuge in the Buddha, the Dhamma and the Sangha.[63]

In his missionary work the Buddha was more successful among the Koliyas than among the Bhaggas. This was due partly to the contiguity of the Koliyas to the Śākyas, and partly to the connection of the Buddha with the Koliyas through his mother and wife. The first visit paid by the Buddha to this country was from Veśāli in the fifth year of his ministry when a fight became imminent between the Śākyas and the Koliyans over the right of drawing water from a stream[64]. It was when the arrives of the two clans were arrayed in the battlefield that the Buddha intervened and brought about an amicable settlement by his thoughtful and pacifying discourses. Many members of both the clans were struck by the Buddha's greatness and were moved so much by his teachings that they retired from the world to become bhikkhus. Of those who were converted to Buddhism at this place, the names of Punnagovatika and Seniya-Kukkuravatika should be mentioned, as they were typical Brāhmaṇic ascetics believing in the efficacy of severe penances.[65]

The prominence attained by the Mallas of Kuśī nārā in the Buddhist literature is due to the accident of Kuśī nārā being the site of Buddha's *parinibbåna.* The reason underlying the objection made by Ananda to the selection of the place by the Buddha for his *parinibbana* was that it was unimportant as a centre of Buddhism.

The Malla country is the scene of two important discourses delivered by the Buddha. One of them in the Sutta is the *Anguthara Nikāya* meant to explain to Tapassu Gahapati the great charm inhering in the spiritual exercises practised by a monk, by virtue of which they could spuru the pleasures of worldly life. It was the attraction of this happiness in the life of a monk that persuaded even youngmen to turn recluses. The Buddha explained the successive stages by which the highest spiritual culture could be reached through this life of meditation and discipline.[66] The other discourse is the Kinti Sutta of the *Majjhima Nikāya* in which the Buddha explained that he was out as a preacher not for any selfish motive but for the spiritual uplift of men who had by previous *Karma* an innate inclination to the attainment of deliverance from the wordly miseries and required some assistance and guidance for the achievement of their object.[67]

AṄGA

In the estimation of the orthodox Brāhmaṇas, Aṅga occupied a place similar to that of Magadha, for it was beyond the Sadānīrā and was looked down upon along with Magadha as a country unfit for the performance of sacrifices and had enough to be a place where fever should be driven away from Brahmasi-deśa.[67] Aṅga like Magadha had renowned Brāhmaṇa teachers, two of whom are mentioned in the Nikāyas. The importance of the country in the history of the spread of Buddhism is on account of its being the easternmost place reached by Buddhism within the Buddha's life-time.[68]

It is not definitely stated anywhere in the Nikāyas and other treatises as to the time when Buddha paid his first visit to the country of Aṅga. On more than one occasion Buddha had been to Aṅga dewelling at Campa, Apana, Assapura and Kajangala. It was during one of these visits that he converted the father-in-law of Anāthpindaka's daughter with other members of his family. During his absence at Campa on this occasion he left Anuraddha to carry on the missionary work.[69] Sonadanda was converted at a time when Bimbisâra, Pasendi and Pokkharasadi had already become the Buddha's disciples. We find that during the Buddha's life time there were at Aṅga several lay devotees, as evidenced not only by passages in the Majjhima and Anguthara Nikāyas[70], but also by separate mentions of their names in various places in the Buddhist scriptures. The Vinaya and the Theragatha supply us with names of a few bhikkhus who were inhabitants of Aṅga.

KĀSĪ

The importance of Kāsi as a great centre of Brāhmaṇic culture and learning is recognised in both the Brāhmaṇic and Buddhistic literature. The frequent mention of the place in the Jātakas is indicative of its great importance in those days. The Rsipattana of Kaso has been immortalised in the Pali as well as the Buddhist Sanskrit literature as a resort of a large number of ṛsis in ancient times. The selection of the locality by the Buddha for the delivery of his first discourse at the commencement of his missionary career is quite in line with its sacred tradition. In this land of othodox Brahmanism, the Buddha's missionary work was naturally hampered by opposition from the Brāhmaṇas. For this reason his success was not so marked as it was in Magadha and Kośala. The Buddha's ministration commenced with the conversion of two foreign traders Trapusa and Bhallika who were travelling with a caravan along the trade route from Dakkhinapath to Ukkala,[71] a town in the kingdom of Gandhara. Their conversion at *Uruvela* was later on commemorated by the erection of stupas in their native villages[72] in Gandhara. The Buddha after enlightenment turned his thoughts first to his comrades in asceticism then residing at Isiptana near Benaras. Here at Isipatna he visited his five comrades who would not accept the Buddha's arguments regarding the futility of extreme self-mortification in taking them to their spiritual goal.

The Buddha accompanied by the five new bhikkhus passed from Isipatna to Benaras and stopped on the bank of the river Varana under a *nigrodh* tree where he met Yasa, a rich settlics son, who had already become sick of this world.

Thus far successful in his mission, the Buddha entertained the idea of spreading his religion far and wide by utilizing the services of these sixty converts as preachers. After sending them to their respective tasks in different places. He himself went to Uruvela for preaching his religion.

VATSA

The Buddha had been to the country of the vatsas on two or three occasions and passed his ninth varsa at Kośāmbī. His tenth varsa was passed in a neighbouring forest called *Parilayyaka* within which he retired in disgust at the quarrel that took place between the two groups of bhikkhus of Kośāmbī, viz, the *Dhammadharas* and the *Vinaydharas.*[73] At Kośāmbī, he usually stayed at the hermitage *Pavarika-ambavana* built by *Pavariya*, a rich settle.

While the Buddha was residing at Kośāmbī he felt the necessity of framing rules for averting chances of future dissensious in his order. He detailed, as recorded in the tenth book of the *Mahavagga,* the circumstances in which a schism could take place and dwelt on their evil consequences.[74]

Apart from these lands, though the whole of western India was placed outside the *majjhima-deśa* of the Vinaya, Buddhism made a fair progress there during the life-time of the Buddha and played an important role in the later history of Buddhism. The religion, however, was not confined to the region, as supposed by Dr. Oldenberg, but spread over many regions of western India.

Even outside India, Buddhism did flourish in other Asian countries, viz. China, Japan and Thailand. In Thailand, Buddhism has largely attracted the Thai people and they still follow the rules framed by the Buddha. But keeping in mind the limitations of a work, the countries outside India may not be included here because it is a matter of separate and extensive study.

REFERENCE

1. *Majjh. Nik.* II. p. 2.
2. Dr. Barua's, *Pre–Buddhistic Indian Philosophy,* p. 281.
3. N. Dutta, Early history of the spread of Buddhism and the Buddhist Schools ; p. 40.
4. *Digh. Nik.* I. p. 117 ff; *Sam. Nik* . I. pp. 172, 173. *Sutta Nipāta,* p. 13.
5. *Sam. Nik.* I. p. 114.
6. *Sutta Nipāta.* p. 50.
7. *Avadāna Sataka,* pp. 83 – 84.
8. N. Dutta, *op. cit.,* p. 48.

the Buddhist pitakas declare them as Buddhists. Neither the Jaina nor the Buddhist literature admits that they were supporters of the religions at different times or at the same time in different degrees. The facts of the lines of the two emperors, however, points to the inference that Bimbisara supported Jainism when it appeared on the field but inclined decidedly towards Buddhism when it asserted itself as a rival of Jainism. Ajatsattu was a supporter of Devadatta who initiated a set holding views similar to Jainism so far as its discipline was concerned. This shows that Devadutta had Jaina sympathies and Ajatsattu by supporting him shows the nature of his religious views. He however, was converted to Buddhism a year before Buddha's parinibbana.

see, V.A. Smith, *Early History of India*, p. 33.

10. N. Dutta, *op. cit* ; p. 51.
11. *Ibid.*
12. *Ibid.*, p. 53.
13. *Ibid.*, p. 56.
14. Sum. Vil., p. 35 *Majjh. Nik.* I.p. 377, *Digh. Nik.* I, *Sutta* II. It is stated in Yuan Chwang's Records and Mahavastu that Nalanda was the birth place of Sariputta, but in fact his birth place was Nalaka which was an unimportant village near Nalanda.
15. *Majjh. Nik.* I, p. 414.
16. *Ibid.* p. 379, Also see, Mahavastu, III, p. 56.
17. Vinay, M.V.VI, p. 28, *Digh. Nik.* II, p. 85.
18. Sutta Nipāta, M. 12ff, Sam. Nik., I. pp. 172 – 73.
19. R.L. Mitra's *Nepalese Buddhist Literature, p.* 18.
20. *Ang. Nik.* IV, p. 63ff.
21. *J.R.A.S.*, 1891, p. 339, Hardy's *Mannual,* p. 356.
22. *Vinaya*, V, pp. 144 – 45.

22. *Vinaya*, V, pp. 144 – 45.

23. Oldenberg's *Buddha*, Appendix – I.

24. *Satpatha Brahmana*, 1. 4, is quoted also in Oldenberg's *Buddha.*, pp. 398 - 399.

25. Mahavastu, III, p. 420; Psalms of the Brethren, p. 284. According to the Buddhist legends, the thirty Bhaddavaggya youths, converted by Buddha on his way from Benaras to uruvela, also belonged to Kośāla (Hardy's Manual of Buddhism p. 188). Buddhaghosa says that the Bhaddvaggya youths were brothers of the king of Kośāla. They after their ordination lived at Patheyya, a country situated to the west of Kośāla. (S.B.E. XVII, p. 146 fn).

26. Watter's *Yuan Chwang*. I. pp. 384-394.

27. *Sam. Nik.* I, p. 68, *Majjh. Nik.* , I., pp. 205, 400, 426.

28. Dr. Berua, *op. cit;* pp. 298, 299, 300.

29. *Sutta Nipata*, pp. 50ff.

30. N. Dutta, *op. cit;* p. 74.

31. *Majjh. Nik.* I, p. 175.

32. *Sutta Nipāta*, p. 21.

33. *Majjh. Nik.* II, p. 209.

34. *Digh. Nik.* II, p. 87.

35. *Ibid*, I.p. 224.

36. Sutta Nipata, p. 192 ff-Bavari was once the purohita of king Mahakośāla and his son Pasendi. He retired to the bank of the Godavari a hemitage was built for him by Pasendi.

37. *Sam. Nik*, I, pp. 75-76; *Sutta Nipāta*, p. 192.

38. *Majjh. Nik.* II, pp. 108, 125-26.

39. *Vinaya*, MT. VIII, 15,7.

40. *Majjh. Nik.* III, p. 1.

41. *Majjh. Nik.* II, p. 23.

42. Hardy's *Manual of Buddhism*, pp. 198ff. Burlingama's *Buddhist legends* II, pp. 2ff.

43. See, Supra, pp. 103-108.

44. *Majj. Nik.* I, pp. 91 - 95.

45. *Ang. Nik.* I.p. 219, III, p. 286.

46. *Ang. Nik.* II, 196 ff.

47. *Ibid* ; V, p. 83.

48. *Majjh. Nik.* I, pp. 358-359.

49. Buddhist India, p. 181 *Sam. Nik.* II, p. 119.

50. *Sam Nik.* I. p. 184.

51. Hardy's *Manual*, p. 356.

52. *Ang. Nik*, II, p. 24, III, p. 169, IV, p. 427, *Sam. Nik.* V, pp. 73, 174, 217.

53. N. Dutta, *op. cit;* p. 85.

54. Dr. B.C. Law, *Ksatriyas clans in Buddhist India*, pp. 88-89.

55. *Digh. Nik.* I, p. 151.

56. *Digh. Nik.* II, p. 102.

58. *Ang. Nik*, IV, p. 274.

59. *Brhadaranyaka Upanishad*, III ; Oldenberg's Buddha, p. 398.

60. *Majjh. Nik*, II, pp. 74 ff, 133 ff.

61. *Ang. Nik*, II, p. 61, III, p. 295, IV, pp. 85, 268.

62. *Majjh. Nik*, I, pp. 95, 332.

63. *Majjh. Nik*, II, p. 91.
64. Burlingam's *Buddhist Legends*, III, pp. 70ff, Jatakas, V, pp. 412-413.

    Hardy's *Manual*, pp. 317-20.
65. *Majjh. Nik*, I, p. 387.
66. *Majjh. Nik*, II, pp. 238-243.
67. *Ibid*, pp. 238-243.
68. *Satpath Brahman*, I, p. 4.
69. Kern's *Manual*, p. 38.
70. *Majjh. Nik*. III, p. 298, *Ang. Nik*. IV, p. 59.
71. *Mahavastu*, III, pp. 324-329 ; *Lalitvistara*, p. 406.
72. *Majjh. Nik*, I, pp. 173-175.
73. N. Dutta, *op.. cit* ; p. 97.
74. *Ibid.* , p. 98.

Conclusion

Although Bihar was not the birth place of Gautama Siddhārtha, yet it happens to be the birth place of Buddhism, which grew into a popular movement. The rise of Buddhism took place at an epoch when not only India but also Greece, Persia and China were experiencing a stir in religious matter through the advent of Socrates with his distinguished people and contemporary philosopher in Greece, of Zoroaster in Persia, and of Lao-tse and Confucius in China. The factors that favoured the origin and spread of early Buddhism in Bihar were not political but geographical also. By the sixth century B.C. iron technology had developed perfectly well in Bihar, which led to the improvement in agricultural methods.

The plenty use of iron in eastern U.P. and north Bihar facilitated the spread of Buddhism the use of iron made it possible to make weapons on the one hand and involved large production on the other. With the use of iron implements deforestation started and the lands were now being brought under cultivation. Vaiśyas were involved in producing activities. The result was surplus production which could maintain surplus population also. When production increased, gradually they grew richer. In this position they could have sought for themselves a position in the society as after the industrial revolution the rising middle class fought for their social status. On the other hand the use of iron helped the warrior class who were in a continuous struggle against the Brāhmaṇas. The Buddha's call for challenging the social hierarchy proved a stimulus to the Kshatriyas. Secondly, Bihar was the land of religious and cultural activities. The real key to the understanding of the rise of new religious movement lies in certain significant development in the material life of the people. Once this newly founded religion saw its origin, it spread at a very fast note. The Vedas involved several Yajñas, which resulted in the killing of animals on a large scale. The Brāhmaṇas were the profiteers in these killings. One interpretation is that Buddhism,which had non-violence and simplicity as its central point became popular as a reaction to the ritual ridden religion of the Vedic people. The Buddha preached that religious truths lay, not in the sacrifices, not in the Vedas which prescribed the sacrifices, not in the worship of many deities of the Brāhmaṇic pantheon but in self-culture culminating in *Arhatship* which constitute the key note of Buddhism. This attracted the people very much. It was this doctrine of *Ahiṁsā* that appeals so much to the heart of the people. Mahāvīrā also launched upon the field of Indian thought before Buddha which is doctrine of *Ahiṁsā* but his followers carried it to such an excess that it could not draw the admiration of the Brāhmaṇas. While the rational view of the same taken by the Buddha attracted the attention of everyone, no matter, whatever creed he might belong to. The Buddha insisted on the moral purity of speech, mind and body for all those who joined the Buddhist order, in and through which the salvation lies. The significance of Nirvāṇa assumes various complexions at the hands of interpreters. But this much is certain that the attainment of the same meant for an individual a permanent escape from the whirling of *Karma* re-birth with their attendant miseries. It can be seen the Buddhism struck out a path of which easiness and simplicity were the characteristic features.

The great stress laid by Buddhism upon the right conduct, so much so that it became one ot its most prominent features, was also an attractive feature.

The commanding personality of the Buddha His self-sacrifice the strength of his character, His spiritual attainments, His supersensual vision and the occasional manifestations served in a great degree to convince the people of His spiritual greatness and made them attach importance to his words.

The character and personality of Buddha's immediate disciples such as Sariputta, Moggalana, Mahākāśyapa and Ānand were also a powerful factor in the propagation of Buddhism. Their excellence have sometimes been mentioned by the Buddha himself.

The Buddhist leaders in the generations following the immediate disciples of Buddha up to the reign of Aśoka included likewise prominent character, who might well take their place by the side of his immediate disciples. These leaders, namely, *Siggava, Sambhuta Sanavastika, Rewat, Yasa, Udena, Upagupta,* etc. Were such monks who took a prominent part in the deliberations of the church organisation and maintained discipline, moral or otherwise.

The rapid spread of Buddhism with in a few centuries after its foundation is due to the fact that conversion of non-Buddhists to Buddhism was regarded as a part of the duty of the monks at the highest stage of their spiritual developments. The sacred books of the Buddhist from the *Nikāyas* downwards contain passages extolling the merits of preaching and conversion.

The political scenario played rather an important role in the origin and spread of any philosophy. The contradiction within the Brāhmaṇism itself appeared to be the most inevitable factor in the rise of Buddhism. Although the socio-economic environment was getting changed with the passage of time, the Brāhmaṇas were not prepared to bring any change in the social hierarchy.

The history of Buddhist art does not really commence until the reign of Asoka, the Great, (Circa 269 B.C.) two centuries and a quarter after the Buddha's nirvāṇa. Under the royal patronage of Asoka, Buddhist art received a forceful fillip and the glorious tradition initiated by him continued up to the times of Ajanta. It does not mean that the Buddhist or Indian art originated in the times of Aśoka. What the Mauryan era signified is the substitution of stone for wood, which was the common material used for building purposes.

Buddhist art is fundamentally art of the people. It reflects the ideas and ideals, ambitions, joys and fears of the Buddhist layman. Although it is essentially religious in character it is nevertheless comprehensive in its scope.

The Buddhist art started in the form of Vihāras, which were used as rest houses by the Buddhist laity. It has been rightly observed that the Buddhist art evolved in answer to a specific demand which was to satisfy the religious urge of the people. The dwelling places of the Bhikṣus in form of Vihāras proved a very valuable centre for propagating the Buddhists faith most effectively. It is learnt form inscriptions at Sanchi and Bharhut that village committees were formed to help building the railings of the stupas at Bharhut and Sanchi.

All Buddhist art could be divided into two distinguished groups. Under the first would fall all such buildings as were utilitarian in purposes, like cells, caves, Vihāras and the other group would comprise commemorative structures like the stupas with their railings. Among the pre-Mauryan art remains of Jarāsandha Ki Baithakā may be mentioned. Parkhām statue of a Yakṣa, two Patna Yakṣa statues, the Besnagar Yakṣi statue and the Besnagar Kalpavrkṣa, etc. are among the pre-Mauryan art remains of India.

With Aśoka the Buddhist Art comes into its own. The teachings of the Buddha served as a great impulse to the development of India art.

Aśokan monuments can be divided into three groups, (1) stupa: (2) cave, and (3) pillar. Although it is an exaggeration to say that Asoka was responsible for building 84000 stupas, yet it cannot be denied that he must have built stupas at various places including the one at Sanchi which happens to belong to the Aśokan age. Sārnāth stupa also belongs to the age of Aśoka.

The earliest historical caves of India can be attributed to the twelefth year of Aśoka. These caves are carved out of a solid piece of rocks, generally of granite. The frontage contains a door with sloping jambs which are evidently a copy of the wooden prototypes. The Lomasa Rishi cave has over its door a carving showing a flowery fringe with another showing a fringe of elephant.

The pillars of Asoka which attract our attention and admiration as monuments of engineering ability, perfect examples of the highest scheme of the stone cutter and vehicles of a brilliant display of fine art, form a distinct landmark in the evolution of Indian architecture and sculpture. These monolithic columns are of highly polished sand stone 30 feet in height.

The relics of Buddhism still existing in Bihar may be divided into five groups: (1) Ruins of caves, (2) Those of monastries orvihāras, (3) Votive stupas, (4) Figures, and sculptures, and (5) Inscriptions. In the field of art no parallel of Didārganj Yakshī of the third century B.C. has yet been found. This stands out as a monumental contribution to the history of world art.

In Aśoka the great Buddhism found a great patron, who played a prominent role in propagating it. It s still controversial whther Aśoka was converted to Buddhism before or after the end of bloody Kaliṇga war. What is beyond controversy is this that the results of Kaliṇga war proved heart rending for Aśoka and that he had a definite role in championing the cause of Buddhism. The Kaliṇga war was an epoch making event, which made him announce a new foreign policy and laid him to think of promotion of *Dhamm.* In the first instance he took the extensive tour of the places connected with Buddhism, which demonstrated his respect for the cult. Firstly, he went on a pilgrimage to Sambodhi (Bodh-Gayā) in the tenth year of his conversion. It may be that after pilgrimage to Bodh-Gaya Aśoka set out on the propagation of his *Dhamma.* Similarly he went to Lumbini, Sārnāth and other places which were of importance to Buddhism. By the time of Aśoka the *Dhamma* had become a strong popular movement and it was strategic for him to have won their confidence. Therefore, he adopted *Dhamma* as an article of faith, when he visited Lumbini after twenty years of his coronation, he offered worship and erected a stone pillar.

In pursuance with the declaration of Buddhism that killing should not be allowed and that non-violence is of vital importance Aśoka ordered that not more than three peacocks would be killed in the royal kitchen and that the festival *samāja* which involved the killing of a large number of birds and animals was effectively banned.

Aśoka was for both political and religious reasons anxious to see that unity in the large and influential Buddhist church is maintained. In order to thrash out the differences, Aśoka convened the third Buddhist council at Pātaliputra which finally settled the rules of discipline and Maggaliputta composed the kathāvatthu. The Buddhists council was intended to ensure unity and cohesion among the Buddhist S. According to the inscriptions also Aśoka was responsible for the spread of Buddhism all over India.

The period intervening between the fall of the Mauryas and the rise of the Kaniṣka group of the Kuṣāṇa kings is of noted importance for two reasons. Firstly, it represented a phase of transition in Indian history. The Mauryan empire after Aśoka the great was shattered. He left no stone unturned to see that Buddhism became popularly acceptable with the masses. After him-India was under the royal sceptie of the Śungas, who immortised themselves for the act of reviving the Brāhmaṇical glory. Now Brāhmaṇism and Buddhism stood against each other. But contrary to what has been described in the Buddhist literature including the *Divyāvadāna,* it was under patronage of puśyamitra that the stupas of Bharhut and Sanchi were built. Assuming that he did not extend his patronage, there is no denying that Vidisā, where Bharhut fell, lay within the territorial jurisdiction of the Śuṅga empire. The famous Buddhist Stupa of Sanchi was also built up during his times. He was no doubt an opponent of Buddhism, but not its persecutor. No doubt this was a period of transition for Buddhism. But it was not persecuted by Puśyamitra Śuṅga or any of his successor as sought to be painted by the overzealous Buddhist literature. Absence of royal patronage does never mean opposition or resistance to the cult.

From the time of Kaniṣka ownwards the cult of Buddha, i.e., Buddhism had to pass through a phase of transformation, from *Sarvāstivāda to Sthavirvavāda* to *Mahasaṁghika,* then to Hinyāna and finally to the Mahāyāna. It was, therefore, a long journey of change for Buddhism. The dissension and further transformation that took place in Buddhism was not peculiarly a strange phenomenon. The Buddha himself had the idea of the ensuing period, when his philosohy would be transformed and it would be divided into many schools. Once Bimbisāra the king of Magadha and a contemporary of the Buddha saw in a dream of a piece of cloth and a stick divided into eighteen fragments. The Buddha is said to have explained that these eighteen fragments represented the eighteen schools into which his philosophy would be divided. Although Aśoka initially succeeded in uniting the various warring groups who were not ready to accept the rules of discipline. After him there was no royal patron and there was no enthusiastic champion of Buddhism who could contain them. The warring factions of the Buddhism who all stood for different philosophies. While Hinayāna advocates liberation from the cycle of life and death and says that one becomes an *arhat.* Only after he individually becomes free from the Bodhisallua ideal is a great land mark in the transformation of life and death. The followers of the Theravāda doctrine based on the Pali text are known as the Hinayānism. The Mahāsaṅghikas who separated themselves from the Theravādins were the pioneers of Mahāyāna movement. The Mahāyānists cherish for the Buddhahood and believed that the Buddhas are *lokottara-supermundane.* The ideal of the Mahāyāna is Buddhahood for all. It assures that perfection can be attained by all. The ideal of the Hinyānist Arhatship which is attainable by a few through practice of discipline prescribed by the Buddha, conception of Buddhism. Mahāyāna has its greatest appeal to the common masses only because of his ideal of sacrifice for the good and happiness of all. This is how Buddhism passed from phase to phase and ultimately changed over to Mahāyānism which had a real appeal to the masses. Although it split up into many schools during the Gupta and post-Gupta period, it was the Mahāyāna alonc which had broad appeal to the masses. From the foregoing passages it becomes clear that Bihar has played a revolutionary role in the origin, spread and development of Buddhism. It was here in Bihar that many important activities took place which shaped the course of Buddhism according to the urge of people.

Bibliography

ORIGINAL SOURCES-TEXTS AND TRANSLATIONS

Aitareya Upaniṣad, ed. Wasudeva Lakshman Shastri Pansikar, 7th ed., Bombay, 1930.

Aṅguttara Nikāya, (Trans.) *The Book of Gradual Sayings,* F.L. Woodward, vols. I to III, London, 1932-33.

Bhagavadgitā, Gita Press, Gorakhpur.

Bodhicaryāvatāra of Śāntideva, ed. P.L. Vaidya, BST, No. 12, 1960.

Bodhisattva-a vadāna-Kalpalatā of kshemendro ed., S.C. Das and H.M. Vidyabhusan, Calcutta, 1888.

Brahmasūtra-Śaṅkara-Bhāṣyam, ed. N.R. Acharya, 3rd ed, Bombay, 1948.

Buddhaghosacariya-(Text) part II, J.H. Woods & D. Kosambi, Part III-V & I. B. Horner, London, 1928-1938.

Buddhist Suttas-Trans. from the Pāli by T.W. Rhys Davids, Oxford, 1887.

Corpus Inscriptionum Indiacarum, Vol. 1, *Aśokan Inscriptions,* Hultzsch, Oxford, 1925; vol. II Pt. I; *Kharoṣti Inscriptions,* Sten Konow, Calcutta, 1929; Vol. II, Pt. II, *Bharhut Inscriptions* (Luders) Ernst Waldschmidt and Mehendale, Cotacamund, 1963.

Cullavagga, ed., J. Kashyap, Nālandā, 1956.

Dhammapada, ed. J. Kashyap in *Khuddaka Nikāya,* Vol. I, Nalanda, 1959.

Dhammapada-Atthakathā (Trans.) Buddhist Legends, Parts I-III, E.W. Burlingame, Mass. Cambridge, 1921.

Dhammasaṅgaṇi: ed. , J. Kashyap, Nālandā, 1960. *Buddhist Psychological Ethics,* Eng. tr. by C.A.F. Rhys Davids, PTS, London, 1909.

Dīgha Nikāya, ed., J. Kashyap, 5 Vols., Nalanda 1960, Hindi tr. by Rahul Sankrityayana, Sarnath, 1936. *Dialogues of the Buddha,* Eng. tr. by T.W. and C.A.F. Rhys Davids, SBB, Vols, 2, 3, 4, London, 1899-1921.

Dīpavaṁśa, ed. and tr. by B.C. Law, *The Ceylon Historical Journal,* Vol. VII, No. 1-4, 1957-58, Also ed. Oldenberg, London 1978.

Divyāvadāna, ed., P.L. Vaidya, BST, No. 20, Darbhanga, 1959

Gilgit Manuscripts, Vol. I, ed., N. Dutt, Srinagar, 1954

I-tsing, A Record of the Buddhist Religion as practised in India and the Malaya Archipelago, Eng., tr. by J. Takakusu, Reprint, Delhi, 1961.

Jain Sūtras, Eng. tr. by H. Jacobi, 2 Pts., SBE, Vols. 22, 45, London, 1884, 1895; Reprint, Delhi, 1964.

Jātaka, ed., J. Kashyap in *Khuddaka Nikāya,* Vol. III. Pts. I-II, Nalanda, 1959, *Buddhist Birth Stories,* ed., and tr. by V. Fausbol, 6, Vols., London, 1895-1913.

Katha Upaniṣad, Gita Press, Gorakhpur.

Kathāvatthu, ed., J. Kashyap, Nālandā, 1961, *Points of Controversy,* Eng. tr. by S.Z. Aung and C.A.F. Rhys Davids, PTS., London, Reprint, 1960.

Mahābodhivaṁśa, PTS, ed.

Mahāvagga, ed, J. Kashyap, Nālandā, 1956.

Mahāvaṁśa, ed., N.K. Bhagwat, 2nd ed,. Bombay, 1959, Eng. tr. by W. Geiger, PTS, London, 1912.

Mahāvāstu, ed., J.P. Minaev, BB, Vol. XIII, St, Petersburg, 1911.

Majjhima Nikāya, (Text) Vols, I-Treckner: II-III-R. Chalmers; IV-V-Mrs. Rhys Davids, London, 1888-1925.

Majjhima Nikāya-(Trans.) *Further Dialogues of the Buddha*, Lord Chalmers, Vols I-II, London, 1926-1927.

Manorathapurani-(Test) Buddhaghosha's Commentary on the Anguttara Nikaya, Vols. I-III, Max Walleser & Herman Kopp, London,1924-1936.

Manusmriti-Ed. by P.H. Pandya, Bombay, 1913. Trans. by G. Buhler, S.B.E., XXV, Oxford, 1886.

Milindapañha (-0), ed., R.D. Vedakar, Bombay, 1940, *Question of King Milinda*, Eng. tr. by T.W. Rhys Davids, 2 Vols., SBE, Reprint, Varanasi, 1965.

Psalms of Early Buddhists, Eng. tr. of *Therīgāthā* and *Theragāthā* by C.A.F. Rhys Davids, 2 Vols., PTS, London, 1909-1913.

Record of Buddhist Kingdoms-Being an account of the Chinese Monk Fa-hien's Travels, Eng. tr. J.A. Legge, Oxford, 1896.

Ṛgvedasamhitā with Commentary of Sāyaṇa, ed. F. Maxmuller, 5 Vols., London, 1849-1874.

Samantapasadika-(Text) Buddhaghosa's Commentary on the Vinaya Pitaka J. Takakusu & M. Nagai Vol. I-V, London, 1924-1938.

Samyutta Nikāya-(Text) M. Leon Feer. Parts I-IV, London, 1884-1894.

Samyutta Nikāya, (Trans.) *The Book of Kindred Sayings*, Eng. tr. by C.A..F. Rhys Davids and F.L. Woodward, 5 Vols., PTS, London, 1917-30.

Śatapatha Brāhmaṇa, ed.,V.S. Ganda, C. Sharma and S.V. Shastri, 2 Vols., Varanasi, 1925-1937.

Si-yu-ki or *Buddhist record of the western world* by Hiuen Tsang, Eng. tr. by S. Beal, 4 Pts., Reprint, Calcutta, 1957.

Sutta-Nipāta, ed. J. Kashyap in *Khuddaka Nikāya*, Vol. I, Nalanda, 1959. *Buddha's Teachings*, ed. and tr. by L. Chalmers, HOS, Vol, XXXVII, London, 1932.

Taittriya Upaniṣad, Gita Press, Gorakhpur.

Tāranātha, *Geschite des Buddhismus*, German tr. by Schiefner, St. Petersburg, 1869.

The Travels of Fa-hien (399-414 A.D.) or *Record of the Buddhistic Kingdom*, Eng. tr. by H.A. Giles, Cambridge, 1923.

Vinaya Pitaka, ed., H. Oldenberg, 5 Vols., London, 1879-1883;

Vinay Texts, Partially tr. by T.W. Rhys Davids and H. Oldenberg, 3 Vols., SBE, Reprint, Varanasi, 1965.

Viṣṇu Purāṇa -Ed. and Trans. by Sri M. Gupta, Gorakhpur, 1936, Trans. by N. Wilson, Vols., I-IV, London, 1864-1874.

Visuddhi-Magga of Buddhaghoṣa- (Test) Vols.I-II, C.A.F. Rhys Davids, London, 1920-1921.

DICTIONARIES AND HISTORY OF PALI LITERATURE

Childers, R.C., *Dictionary of Pali*, London, 1909.

Franke, R.O., *Pali and Sanskrit*, Strassburg, 1902.

Geiger, W. *Pali Literature and Sprache*, Strassburg, 1902.

Law, B.C., *History of Pali Literature,* Vols. I-II, London.

Malalasekera, G.P. *Dictionary of Pali Proper Names,* Vols. I-II, London, 1937-1938.

Max Muller-Ancient Sanskrit Literature.

Rhys Davids, T.W. & W. Stede, *Dictionary of Pali,* London, 1925.

Winternitz, M., *History of Indian Literature,* Vol. II-*Buddhist & Jaine Literature,* Calcutta, 1933.

BOOKS

Agrawal, V.S., *India as known to Panini,* Lucknow, 1953.

Bachhofer, *Early Indian Sculpture.*

Bapat, P.V., (ed.) *2500 years of Buddhism,* Publication Division, Delhi, 1956, Reprint, 1959.

Barua, B.M. *A History of Pre-Buddhistic Indian Philosophy,* Calcutta, 1921.

Barua, B.M. & Sinha, G., *Bharhut Inscriptions,* Calcutta, 1926.

Basham, A.L. *A new study of the Sakā Kushana period,* BOSAS, 1953.

Basham, A.L., *The wonder that was India,* London, 1954.

Bhandarkar, D.R. *Aśoka,* 3rd ed., Calcutta, 1955.

Bhattacarya, . B. , *Indian Buddhist Iconography,* Oxford University Press, 1924.

Bhattacarya, V., *The Basic Conception of Buddhism,* Calcutta, 1934.

Broadley, A.M. *The Buddhistic Remains of Bihar,* Varanasi, 1979.

Buchanan, H, *An açcount of the District of Bihar and Patna.*

Burgess, J, *Buddhistic Art in India,* London, 1901.

Conz, Edward., *Buddhism its Essence and Development,* London, 1951.

Coomarswamy, A, *Buddhism and Gospel of Buddhism,* London, 1927.

Coomarswamy, A., *Introduction to Indian Art.*

Copleston, R.S., *Buddhism, Primitive and Present in Magadha and Ceylon,* London, 1892.

Cunningham, A., *Mahābodhi,* London, 1892.

Dahlke, P., *Buddhist Essays,* London, 1908.

De, Gokul Das., *Democracy in early Buddhist Samgha,* Calcutta, 1955.

Dhar. S., *Transformation and Trend of Buddhism in the 20th century,* Calcutta, 1986.

Dutt, N.K., *Early History of the Spread of Buddhism and the Buddhist Schools,* New Delhi, 1980.

Dutt, N.K. *Early Monastic Buddhism,* 2 Vols., Calcutta, 1941-45.

Edkins, Joseph., *Chinese Buddhism, Chaukhamba,* 1975.

Eliot, Charles., *Hinduism and Buddhism,* Vols. I-II, London, 1921.

Fergusson & Burgess, *Cave Temples of India.*

Fergusson, J., *History of Indian Eastern Architecture* , Vols. I-II, London, 1910.

Fick, Dr. R., *Die Sociale G. Lie derung etc.* Trans. by Dr. S.K. Maitra.

Foucher, A., *The Beginnings of Buddhist Art,* London, 1917.

Gangoly, O.C. , *The Antiquity of the Buddha Image. The cult of the Buddha,* Souderabzug aus osta.

Gokhale, B.G., *Buddhism and Aśoka,* Bombay, 1949.

Gour, Sir H.S., *The Spirit of Buddhism,* London, 1929.

Grierson, G.A., *Notes on the District of Gaya,* Calcutta, 1893.

Grunwedel, A., *Buddhist Art in India,* London, 1901.

Hastings, *Encyclopaedia of Religion and Ethics.*

Havell, E.B., *A Handbook of Indian Art,* London, 1920.

Havell, E.B., *Ideals of Indian Art,* London, 1920.

Havell, E.B., *Indian Architecture* , London, 1913.

Hopkins, E.W., *Religion of India: Handbook on the History of Religions,* Boston, 1895.

Horner, I.B. *The Early Buddhist Theory of Man Perfected,* London, 1936.

Hultzsch, *Inscriptions of Aśoka,* C.I.I., Vol. I, Oxford, 1925.

Humphreys, Christmas., *Buddhism,* Penguin Books, 1951.

Jain, Bhagchandra, *Baudha Samskriti Ka Itihas,* (Hn.) Nagpur, 1972.

Jayaswal, *Manu and Yadnyavalkya.*

Joshi, L.M., *Studies in the Buddhistic Culture of India,* Banaras, 1967.

Junjiro, Takakusu., *The Essential of Buddhist Philosophy,* University of Hawaii,1949.

Keith, A.B. *Buddhist Philosophy in India and Ceylon,* Oxford, 1923.

Kern, H., *Manual of Indian Buddhism,* Strassburg, 1896. Reprint, Varanasi, 1968.

Kimura, R., *An Historical study of the terms Hīnyana and Mahāyāna and the Origin of Mahāyāna Buddhism,* Calcutta, 1927.

Kimura, R., *Original and Developed Doctrines.*

Kosambi, D.D., *Bhagavān Buddha,* Trans. from Marathi into Hindi, Shripad Joshi, Delhi, 1956.

Kosambi, D.D., *Introduction to the study of Indian History,* Bombay, 1956.

Law, B.C., (ed.) *Buddhistic Studies,* Calcutta, 1952.

Law, B.C., *Concepts of Buddhism,* 2nd ed., Leiden, 1966.

Law, B.C. *Geography of Early Buddhism,* London, 1932, Reprint, Varanasi, 1973.

Malalasekera, G.P., *Encyclopaedia of Buddhism,* Vol. I, Fas, 1-4, Vol. II, Fas. I, 1961.

Marshall , Sir John., *The Monuments of Sanchi,* 3 Vols. Reprint Delhi, 1940.

Mathur. J.C. & Mishra, Y., (ed.) *Homage to Vaisali,* (Vaisali Abhinandan Grantha), Vaisali Sangha, 1948.*

McCrindle, J.W., *Ancient India,* Calcutta, 1902.

Mehta, R.N., *Pre Buddhist India,* Bombay, 1939

Mishra, Y., Asoka, Patna 1965, Second Revised edition, 1994.

Mitra, R.L., *Bodh-Gaya, the Hermitage of Śākyamuni,* Calcutta, 1978.

Mookerji, R.K., *Aśoka,* London, 1928.

Mookerji, R.K., *Men and Thought*

Mukherjee, Sat Rani., *The Cultural Heritage of India.*

Murti, T.R.V., *The Central Philosophy of Buddhism,* 2nd ed. London,

Nikam, K.A. and Mekeon, R. *The Edicts of Aśoka,* Chicago, 1959.

Obermiller, E. Buston's., *History of Buddhism.* Pts. I-II, Heidelberg, 1931-32.

Oldenburg's, H., *Buddha,* Eng. Trans. by W. Hoey, Calcutta, 1882.

*Second enlarged edition, Vaisali Prakrit Research Institute, 1985

Pande, G.C., *Studies in the Origins of Buddhism,* 2nd ed. Delhi, 1974.

Pandeya, Ramchandra., (ed.) *Buddhist Studies in India,* Delhi, 1975.

Patil, D.R., *The Antiquarian remains of Bihar,* Patna, K.P. Jayaswal Research Institute, 1963.

Pischel, R,. *Leban and Lehre des Buddha,* Leipzig, 1918.

Przyluski, J., '*Uposatha*', *Journal of Buddhist India,* 1927.

Puri, B.N., *India Under the Kushanas,* Bombay, 1965.

Radhakrishnan, S., *Gautama the Buddha,* Bombay, 1945.

Radhakrishnan, S. *Inidan Philosophy,* 2 Vols. Reprint, 1951.

Rahul Sankrityan., *Buddhism : Marxist Approach,* IV ed., New Delhi, 1985.

Rahul, Walpola, *What the Buddha Taught,* New York, 1962.

Raychoudhry, H.C., *Political History of Ancient India,* 6th ed., Calcutta, 1953.

Rhys Davids., *Buddhist India,* London, 1971.

Rhys Davids. *Hibbert Lectures-Lectures on the Growth of Religion Indian Buddhism,* Reprint, Allahabad, 1972.

Rhys Davids, T.W. *Early Buddhism,* London, 1914.

Rhys Davids, *Buddhism, its History and Literature,* New York, 1896.

Rockhill, W.W., *Life of the Buddha,* London, 1884.

Sankelia, H.D., *Buddhist Ideals,* Calcutta, 1912.

Sankelia, H.D., *Gautama Buddha,* Calcutta, 1929.

Sharma, R.S., *Material Culture and Social formation in Ancient India,* Delhi, 1983.

Sinha, B.P., *Bhartiya Kala ko Bihar Ki Den.*

Smith, V.A., *Asoka, The Buddhist Emperor of India*, Oxford, 1920.

Smith, V.A., *Greek Art and National life.*

Sogen, Y., Systems of *Buddhist Thought*, Calcutta, 1912.

Stcherbatsky, Th., *The Conception of Buddhist Nirvana*, Leningrad, 1927.

Suzuki, D.T., *Outline of Mahayana Buddhism*, Luzac & Co. London, 1907.

Tāranath, *The Chronology of the Reign of Asoka*, St. Petersburg, 1869.

Thakur, A.L., *Comprehensive History of Bihar*, (ed.) Vol. I, Part I, Patna, 1974.

Thapar, Romila, *Aśoka and Decline of the Mauryas*, Delhi, 1973.

Thomas, E.J. *Early Buddhist Scriptures*, London, 1935.

Thomas, E.J., *The History of Buddhist Thought*, London, 1933.

Tripathi, H., *Baudhadharma Aur Bihar*, Panta, 1960.

Vogel, J. Ph., *Buddhist Art in India, Ceylon and Java*, London, 1926.

Wagel, Narendra, *Indian Buddhism*, Delhi, 1970.

Wagel, Narendra, *Society at the time of the Buddha*, Bombay, 1966.

Waren, H.C., *Buddhism* in Translation, Harvard University Press, 1922.

Williams, Monier, *Buddhism in its conception with Brahmanism and Hinduism*, London, 1889.

Williams, Sir M.M., *Buddhism*, Varanasi, 1964.

Wilson, H.H., *Buddha and Buddhism*, London, 1872.

Index